Studies in African American History and Culture

Edited by
Graham Hodges
Colgate University

A Routledge Series

STUDIES IN AFRICAN AMERICAN HISTORY AND CULTURE

GRAHAM HODGES, *General Editor*

RACE AND MASCULINITY IN CONTEMPORARY AMERICAN PRISON NARRATIVES

Auli Ek

Routledge
Taylor & Francis Group
New York London

Published in 2005 by
Routledge
Taylor & Francis Group
711 Third Avenue
New York, NY 10017

Published in Great Britain by
Routledge
Taylor & Francis Group
2 Park Square
Milton Park, Abingdon
Oxon OX14 4RN

First issued in paperback 2013

International Standard Book Number-10: 0-415-97570-0 (Hardcover)
International Standard Book Number-13:978-0-415-97570-4(Hardcover)
International Standard Book Number-13: 978-0-415-65127-1 (Paperback)

Library of Congress Card Number 2005011571

Library of Congress Cataloging-In-Publication Data

Ek, Auli, 1955-
    Race and masculinity in contemporary American prison narratives / Auli Ek.
        p. cm. -- (Studies in African American history & culture)
    Includes bibliographical references (p.   ) and index.
    ISBN 0-415-97570-0 (acid-free paper)
    1. American prose literature--20th century--History and criticism. 2. Prisoners in literature. 3. African American prisoners--Biography--History and criticism. 4. Prisoners' writings, American--History and criticism. 5. Narration (Rhetoric)--History--20th century. 6. Difference (Psychology) in literature. 7. Masculinity in literature. 8. Prisons in literature. 9. Race in literature. 10. Men in literature. I. Title. II. Studies in African American history and culture.

PS366.P75E38 2005
818'.409--dc22
                          2005011571

Routledge
Taylor & Francis Group
New York   London

Visit the Taylor & Francis Web site at
http://www.taylorandfrancis.com

and the Routledge Web site at
http://www.routledge-ny.com

To my family—rakkailleni

Contents

Acknowledgments

I would like to thank my dissertation committee—Carl Gutiérrez-Jones, Maurizia Boscagli, and Alycee Lane—for sharing their expertise and for providing an enormous amount of support throughout my work. I also want to thank Laurel Bush at the University of Helsinki for encouraging me to apply for the American Council of Learned Societies fellowship that enabled me to begin my research in the United States. I am grateful to the Academy of Finland and the Department of English, Writing Program, and Center for Chicano Studies at the University of California, Santa Barbara for funding my project. Special thanks are due to Susan Najita, who commented on my work at the most crucial moments, and to the following friends, colleagues, and professors who encouraged, assisted, and inspired me at various stages of my work: Elliott Butler-Evans, Marc Coronado, Shirley Geok-lin Lim, Tiina Itkonen, Kathy Patterson, Constance Penley, Kimberley Snow, María Herrera-Sobek, Barry Spacks, Dave Vazquez, and Candace Waid in Santa Barbara, and Pekka Kuusisto, Mark Shackleton, Tuire Valkeakari, and Jan-Ola Östman in Helsinki. I also want to remember my parents, Raili and Ole Ek, who have always remained supportive, and—most importantly—Keith Garrett, who gave me peace of mind and heart, and the strength I needed to go on.

Introduction

Representing Criminals

Because prisons are an intrinsic part of contemporary American culture, a wide range of cultural products feeds the popular imaginary with representations of life in prison. The contemporary visual media is particularly productive in generating narratives that satisfy the audience's fascination with stories about dangerous men (and increasingly also women) in prison.[1] The sexy prison "cool" of Elvis Presley's "Jailhouse Rock" from the 1950s has been reincarnated in the lyrics and the baggy pants of hip hop culture; television shows such as ABC's Ted Koppel's "Crime and Punishment" report on the latest high-tech developments in prison architecture; films like *American History X* illustrate the reconfigurations of interracial relations in the context of prison; "true crime" stories provide insight into the psychology of the criminal mind; and classic comedies like *Stir Crazy* and more recent filmic narratives such as HBO's *OZ* represent and create notions of violent prison sexuality. Even family-oriented shows such as *The Simpsons* simultaneously ridicule and perpetuate clichéd preconceptions of prison cells as cramped, rat-infested spaces with stinking toilets "just inches from your bed"—close proximity which for Bart, of course, represents a "luxury." Because of the pervasiveness of television shows such as *America's Most Wanted, Cops,* and *Law & Order,* it appears that consumers of American culture are in daily contact with criminals and enjoy watching them get the punishment they deserve. First hand— yet simulated—experience of incarceration can also be gained by visiting institutions like Alcatraz or a local jail that arranges guided tours.[2]

Incarceration is also an immediate personal experience to a vast and rapidly growing number of Americans. In fact, the United States has the largest penal system in the world, with a prison and jail population of 1,965,495 currently under Federal and State jurisdiction.[3] Including people on parole and probation, the total number of adults under correctional supervision is 6,467,200.[4] The number of people incarcerated in the United

States is projected to continue to grow, and the prison population in 2020 is estimated to be 9,373,427.[5] Statistics also show a gross racial imbalance in the prison population: at midyear 2001, for example, there were 4,848 sentenced black male inmates per 100,000 black males in the United States, 1,668 sentenced Hispanic male inmates per 100,000 Hispanic males, and 705 sentenced white male inmates per 100,000 white males.[6] African American men currently represent about 50 percent of the total prison population, although only 12 to 13 percent of the overall population of the United States is black (Tonry 10, 18). While the number of female prisoners is as low as 6.6 percent of the total prison population,[7] this number is growing at an alarming rate—an increase of 417 percent between 1980 and 1995, compared to a 235 percent increase for men—and the rate of increase is particularly high for African American women (Mauer, *Race* 185, 125).

With these two major trajectories in mind, the real-life experience of prisons and the popular interest in the representations of those experiences, my interdisciplinary project brings together, as a genre in its own right, a body of work that has previously received critical attention only as marginal subgenres of other categories of cultural products: prison autobiographical writing as a subgenre of American autobiography and prison films as a subgenre of "action" or "crime" films, for example. My aim is also to fill a void within humanist approaches to incarceration; although Michel Foucault's *Discipline and Punish: The Birth of the Prison* has influenced a number of humanist scholars since its publication in 1975, there are few works in the areas of literary, film, or media criticism that focus on prison narratives specifically as *prison* narratives.

The most comprehensive work on American prison narratives to date is H. Bruce Franklin's anthology, *Prison Writing in 20th-Century America* (1998). In the introduction to his book, Franklin characterizes modern American prison writing as a "coherent body of literature with a unique historical significance and cultural influence" (1). He traces the history of modern American prison writing to slave songs, which evolved into prison work songs and blues and later into jazz and rock lyrics (8). Franklin delineates the history of American prison narratives by focusing on how major changes in American society coincide with changes in the genre and thematic focus of prison writing. He claims that during the Depression era and the political movements of the 1960s and 1970s, in particular, there developed a "dialectic between the consciousness emerging inside the prison and the forces at work in the larger society" (12). In other words, Franklin suggests that prison narratives not only *reflect* changes in society, but also induce those changes by offering a window through which to look at American society, as if from the outside.

Franklin also discusses the repression of prison literature during the 1980s and 1990s. The political climate of the 1980s no longer favored creative writing courses in prisons or literary journals publishing prison writing and, since then, laws have been passed to make it illegal for prisoners to collect money from their writings (14). "Although ostensibly designed to 'protect the victim' and to keep criminals from profiting from their crimes," Franklin claims, "the real purpose of these laws was identical to the purpose of the repression of prison literature in the 1930s: to keep American people in the dark about the American prison" (14).

Other rare studies on prison narratives are James Massey's *Doing Time in American Prisons: A Study of Modern Novels* (1989), which analyses the works of writers Chester Himes, Malcolm Braly, Edward Bunker, and Nathan C. Heard, and James Robert Parish's *Prison Pictures from Hollywood: Plots, Critiques, Casts and Credits for 293 Theatrical and Made-for-Television Releases* (1991). Another recent anthology is Bell Gale Chevigny's *Doing Time: 25 years of Prison Writing* (1999), which includes texts by fifty male and female inmates. The Canadian based *The Journal of Prisoners on Prisons* publishes texts by prisoners and ex-prisoners written in English and in French and is also exceptional in its focus on scholarly articles rather than creative writing on prisoner experience. Wilbert Rideau and Ron Wikberg's *Life Sentences: Rage and Survival Behind Bars* (1992), written by two prisoners in the Louisiana State Prison in Angola who also are the editors of the award-winning prison news magazine *The Angolite,* is another ambitious work.

In the field of criminology, Michael Tonry's *The Handbook of Crime and Punishment* (1998) includes an impressive collection of texts that analyze a wide range of issues regarding the U.S. criminal justice system, and Christian Parenti's *Lockdown America: Police and Prisons in the Age of Crisis* (1999) offers an exciting and passionate look at the contemporary practices of law enforcement in the United States. In addition to Tonry, several other criminologists take a highly critical view of the political economy of incarceration, particularly during the 1990s, when crime rates were at a record low in the United States.[8] In Vivien Stern's major of critique of mass incarceration, *A Sin Against the Future: Imprisonment in the World* (1998), she argues that imprisonment represents "as big a danger to us in the future as polluting the environment and using up the natural resources of the globe" (xxi). Stern claims that mass incarceration is dangerous—because the imprisoned do not get any better, but worse—and ineffective—because the public does not feel any safer (289).

According to Thomas Mathiesen, in *Prison on Trial: A Critical Assessment* (1990), the "prison does not have a defence, the prison is a fiasco," since it does not fulfill its purposes of individual prevention (for example, rehabilitation, incapacitation, deterrence), of general prevention, or of serving justice (137). Mathiesen (with reference to several other works) therefore explores the ideas of freezing or reducing the size of prisons and partially or fully abolishing them (152). He claims that all of the above methods have been used in the past without "any serious detriment to the population" (153). What Mathiesen suggests as the solution for crime management in the future is increasing the visibility of prisoners in society (163). If prisoners remain invisible to the rest of society, he claims, it is possible for the "ideology of prison" to maintain the present trends; visibility is "the Achilles' heel" of the ideological functioning of the prison (163).

Nils Christie, in *Crime Control as Industry: Towards GULAGS, Western Style* (1994), links the problem of corrections to two conditions containing "potentialities for unrest" in the late-capitalist societies: unequal distribution of wealth and unequal access to paid work (13). Like Mathiesen, Christie claims that the "nearness" of people and the localized control of crime is the answer for crime management: people are less likely to commit crimes against someone they know and also less likely to demand extreme punishments for crimes committed by people they know; they are willing to negotiate (20–23). Christie also describes the growth in the use of imprisonment in the United States as a global threat. He claims that the major threat that crime poses in modern societies like the United States is not the crime itself, but the method of crime control—mass incarceration—because it may lead towards "totalitarian developments" (16). Because of its status as *the* superpower in the world, the United States may influence other countries' penal legislation, and the resultant legislative applications would lead to similar developments in those countries (199).

Criminologists and other scholars have commented on the irrationality of mass imprisonment at a historical moment when crime rates are dropping. According FBI reports, crime in the United States fell for "a record eighth straight year in 1999" (Lichtblau A10). From 1998 to 1999 alone, violent crime fell 10.4 percent and property crime 8.9 percent (Dennis, "Bottoming" 6). It has also been pointed out that the current "tough-on-crime" and "war-on-drugs" policies cannot be the reason for the drop in crime rates, since they have not been in force long enough to cause any significant trend (Tonry, "Harsh" 31). However, the drug wars as "tickets to political success" and "anti-crime one-upmanship" have had the unintended consequence of overburdening of the federal prison system (Dennis, "Federal" 5).

It is in this context of the politicized economy of imprisonment and "war on crime" that my study examines the intersections of the discourses of race, masculinity, and otherness that define prisoner identity in a wide range of prison narratives: from autobiographies, novels, films, documentaries, television shows, and websites to works in the fields of criminology and sociology.[9] My work within the larger approaches of American Studies and Cultural Studies is interdisciplinary, and as such applies theories of literary criticism and visual culture, and methods used in the study of race, genders, and sexualities. My choice of texts is selective; rather than aiming to cover the history of prison narratives as a whole, I focus on certain trends and texts that mark ideological changes within the genre and also reflect simultaneous social and cultural changes in how race, class, gender, and sexuality are perceived to inform identity formation.

As an interdisciplinary project focusing on race, my work participates in the ongoing discussion of the workings of the cultures of race and racism in the United States. Three studies, in particular, have shaped my thinking on these issues: Robyn Wiegman's *American Anatomies: Theorizing Race and Gender* (1995), which critiques the late 20th-century "integrationist aesthetics (both political and representational) [that] emerged as the strategic and contradictory means for reframing and securing the continuity of white supremacy" (116); George Lipsitz's *The Possessive Investment in Whiteness: How White People Profit from Identity Politics* (1998), which discusses whiteness as property and white supremacy as a political choice that does not depend on the race of the person committed to it; and Carl Gutiérrez-Jones' *Critical Race Narratives: A Study of Race, Rhetoric, and Injury* (2001), which criticizes the ideologies of race-blindness in the context of legal discourse.

Prison narratives provide an exceptional source for the study of minority positions—or discourses of otherness—in American culture. The discourse of otherness is central to prison narratives because the narratives both represent prisoner identities constructed as "them"—not "us"—and revise these identities by resisting the ideology of otherness. The "official" prison narratives produced by the criminal justice system and the media, for instance, represent the criminal as the public enemy, an identity that is consistent with the "war on crime" rhetoric. Minority visibility in the media is also particularly pronounced in the context of criminality, where the public fear of crime is intertwined with prejudiced conceptions of the racial other. Prisoner and prison activist-originated narratives, on the other hand, contest the seeming transparency of criminal identity: the logic, for instance, that if the majority of current inmate populations consist of men of color, it follows that criminality is somehow inherent to African American and Latino men.[10] The two main competing discursive modes of prison narratives are, then, the reproduction of popular images of raced and gendered criminal identities and the resistance to these stereotypic and marginalizing representations.

In this study I analyze these two basic modes of representation of prison narratives within the framework of two of Michel Foucault's interrelated theories about discursive technologies of discipline. First, I consider the resistance to the institutionalized discourses and the objectification of prisoners into disciplinary subjects within the framework of Michel Foucault's techniques of "totalizing" and "individualizing" power, as he discusses them in "The Subject and Power." Prison narratives resist the totalizing and individualizing procedures exerted by the "state," or criminal justice system, by foregrounding prisoners' refusal to be classified and categorized based on criminal acts that turn individuals into statistical data. Thus, prison narratives counteract the established logic of imprisonment and promote forms of prisoner subjectivity that transgress those based on de-individualizing criminality. It must be acknowledged, though, that the promotion of new prisoner identities is a complex process in which the narrative choices of prioritizing race, sexuality, or individual success, for example, tend to undermine each other and result in reassessments of criminality that may seem rather compromised.

Michel de Certeau's *The Practice of Everyday Life* (1984), in part as a critique to Foucault's paradigms of knowledge and power, suggests a more nuanced view of the positions of power in terms of resistance. De Certeau's basic classification of positions of power consists of two sectors: "strategic" power exerted by established institutions and "tactics" practiced by individuals. In my application, the institutions of the U.S. criminal justice system and the prison represent the former and prisoner autobiographies that must be "smuggled" out of prisons the latter. As an example of tactical practices, de Certeau cites employees' private work done in the workplace using the employer's tools and materials (25). As Carl Gutiérrez-Jones has pointed out, however, the everyday resistance that employees thus practice may only seems to be empowering resistance; employers may well be aware of what is taking place, but choose not to interfere in order to strengthen their strategic sense of power (*Rethinking*

186, n. 17). In a similar manner, the prison as an institution may appear to turn a blind eye to the publication of autobiographical texts that criticize the system of imprisonment, for instance, but in fact may be controlling it by *allowing* it to happen.

Second, in *The History of Sexuality*, Foucault discusses how heterosexuality became normalized through the discursive systems that define other than heterosexual acts as perversions, so that the notion of heterosexuality as normative behavior depends on the existence of homosexuality as the non-normative. In a similar manner, criminality is defined as the non-normative so that the non-criminal can be perceived as the norm. Discourses of criminality thus structure and legitimize the logic of imprisonment. In the context of sexuality, Foucault also delineates the discursive paradigm shift within which the focus on the "perverse" sexual act is replaced with the focus on the transgressive bodies performing the act. This kind of a shift is also apparent in the modern discursive practices of criminality, particularly within the visual media: the focus on criminality itself has been replaced by the visuality of the criminal other.

In Tim Willocks' novel *Green River Rising* (1994),[11] Warden John Campbell Hobbes refers to the normative function of criminal bodies in the speech that he makes to inmates during a prison uprising. The warden uses a septic tank metaphor to rationalize the existence of prisoners:

> You exist—purely and simply—to provide a filth drain, a septic tank into which the rest of us can excrete our own malice and cruelty, our lust for vengeance, our dark unspoken fantasies of violence and greed. Your pain is essential to the smooth functioning of civilisation. But do not flatter yourselves. Your individual crimes—no matter how shocking—have no meaning whatsoever. All that is required is that you be here, innocent or guilty, good an bad alike. You are the pot to be shat in—that and nothing more . . . just by being here you are doing excellent service—a good job—for the society you so despise. (8–9)

Besides expressing a view of imprisonment that objectifies prisoners as commodities used for purposes other than actual punishment, Warden Hobbes also names prisoners as the other, whose very existence boosts the moral superiority of law-abiding citizens. As the "pots to be shat in," prisoners represent something even lower than society's excrement. Prison narratives thus typically represent prisoners in terms of the "low"—in terms of social, moral, and sexual deviance—metaphorized and fetishized through the narrative focus on dirt, bodily functions, violence, and sexual perversion.

In *The Politics and Poetics of Transgression* (1986), Peter Stallybrass and Allon White analyze the manner in which the cultural categories of "high" and "low"—social and aesthetic—organize subjectivity through the difference they establish: "each extremity structures the other, depends upon and invades the other in certain historical moments, to carry political change through aesthetic and moral polarities" (3–4). As "high discourses," Stallybrass and White identify, for instance, "literature, philosophy, [and] statecraft," and, as "low discourses," the discourses of "the urban poor, subcultures, [and] marginals" (4). They also acknowledge that the higher discourses are "normally associated with the most powerful socio-economic groups," and therefore generally have the authority to define what is high and low in a society (4). In the example of Tim Willocks' *Green River Rising*, Warden Hobbes asserts his authority in this sense. As the representative of the "official" or "high" discourse of imprisonment, he exerts the power to define prisoners as the "low"—as human "filth drains," and as individuals whose crimes "have no meaning whatsoever" (8–9).

The ideological constructions of cultural and social difference that Stallybrass and White outline with reference to Victorian London—with its extremes of upper class neighborhoods and slums, gentlemen and prostitutes—apply particularly well to the cultural and social implications expressed by prison narratives. Representing a subculture, marginality, and the urban poor, prison narratives both reinforce and resist the categories of the social and aesthetic high and low. It is safe to assume that prison narratives as a genre have received little critical notice until recently because they are considered to represent a low aesthetic enterprise. This evaluative tendency may be the reason why prison narratives, as a subculture regarded as marginal because of its subject matter and narrative focus, often aim at including discursive strategies of the "high" in order to be recognized as aesthetically relevant.

From the perspective of *social* high and low, prison narratives work as an agent for establishing moral polarities for identity formation, but prison narratives also themselves re-establish the categories of high and low within the social hierarchies of prisons. The polarities reappear when the narratives re-categorize prisoners in order to establish who the "real" criminal is. In "escape-from" prison films, for instance, the white male is typically not depicted to be as criminal as his fellow inmates who are African American or Latino. Thus, there is no "outside" within the symbolical representation of cultural categories of high and low; as Stallybrass and White put it, the categories "invade" each other (3).

Another way to look at prison narratives invading a cultural space, and creating the difference between the self and the other, is to consider the ambiguous way these narratives both evoke repugnance and fascination in their audience. Stallybrass and White claim that the low symbolically represents the "primary erotiziced constituent" of the "fantasy life" of the high, so that the high not only depends on the low, but also includes it (5). Thus the criminal bodies that fascinate the audience of the visual media provide a privileged position from which to observe the life that does not seemingly represent the self, and to simultaneously embrace the fantasy of occupying the locus of the criminal—the demonized and desired other. Although prisoners as the criminal class may be considered socially peripheral, prison narratives—through the "mobile, conflictual fusion of power, fear and desire" that they offer—are symbolically central as the moral and aesthetic other that structures the American social and cultural self (5).[12]

Besides serving as the discursive release valve for the American cultural imaginary, prisoners are commodified in more concrete ways as well. According to the criminologist Nils Christie, imprisonment in the United Stated has evolved into an industry, the purpose of which is the control and management of the "dangerous classes" of society, which in turn provide an endless amount of "raw material" for the operation of the prison industrial complex (69, 116).[13] The expansion of imprisonment into an industry that is managed as a profitable business in a capitalist economy has turned prisoners into objects that are housed in experimental, highly technologically oriented units, where little of no attention is given to rehabilitative methods.[14] The privatization of prisons, in particular, furthers the ideology of prisoners as commodities to be stored for long periods of time, at as little expense as possible. Some facilities also use prisoners to create a new kind of a working class.[15] Although employment is seen as a privilege by inmates of the "post-correction age"—primarily because it makes serving time easier—capitalizing work done far below minimal wages raises ethical questions, and is also a security concern for consumers whose personal information is available to inmates working for credit card companies, for example.

In a political climate in which incarceration is regarded as higher education in criminality rather than punishment that reforms criminal behavior and in which 67 percent of law-enforcement officials do not believe that capital punishment reduces the homicide rate,[16] the only sense the massive expansion of imprisonment makes is business sense. In *Going Up the River: Travels in a Prison Nation* (2001), Joseph Hallinan discusses the rationale of U.S. prison system in terms of profitable businesses and a "pay less" working class in prisons. He writes that facilities like the Eastern Oregon Correctional Institution pay its inmates "pretty good money—$6.25 an hour"—and still manage to make profit as "Inside Oregon Enterprises" (143). The trick is that, although the inmates are paid market wages, "employers offer no retirement, vacation, or health benefits; nor do they pay Social Security, workers' compensation, or Medicare," and therefore can cut the employer's payroll costs by 35 percent (143–144). This kind of state-legislated policy places the average working-class citizens in double jeopardy: their tax money covers the housing of the inmates whose employment in prison obliterates job opportunities on the outside. In addition to the conflict of interests between working classes in and outside of prisons, privileging inmates as the more desirable work force also means "a degree of power" for them, as Nils Christie points out, and "could mean trouble ahead for authorities" in the future of corrections (74).[17]

The ethical questions raised by the commodification of prisoners and the privatization of the prison industry is reflected in the pessimistic vision of narratives predicting the future of imprisonment in the United States. These narratives—generally science fiction films—primarily focus on imprisonment from the point of view of a global economy that prioritizes business interests over human rights: national citizenships are replaced by global prisonerships and prisoner bodies—male prisoners as work force or as material for experimentation and female prisoners for reproductive purposes—are sold to private enterprises. In other words, these narratives suggest that, in the future criminal justice system, there will be no pretense of justice being done and that any deed could be criminalized in order to secure the uninterrupted supply of fresh raw material for the prison industry.

Since the current war on crime, and the war on drugs in particular, targets the kinds of crimes not typically committed by members of the affluent sections of society, today's incarceration rates also are a function of the prisoners' social class. Marc Mauer, in *Race to Incarcerate* (1999), discusses how the lack of education, low income, and unemployment—together with race—correlate with high incarceration rates. In public discourses on crime, race is the factor highlighted, while the issue of poverty is overlooked.[18] As an example, Mauer discusses legislation that targets the use and sale of crack cocaine and simultaneously offers more lenient punishments for crimes related to powder cocaine, the drug favored by wealthy users (154–157). Besides being searched and arrested for drug offenses more often than whites, urban and poor blacks and Latinos are also more likely to make an income selling drugs (165, 167). According to Mauer, young African American and Latino males who are unemployed because their education is below high school diploma level resort to crime because of poverty more than other factors (162). Urban and poor minority neighborhoods are also often identified as criminal: "ghettos and no-go areas are seen as the breeding grounds of crime and criminals" (Bauman 125).

Race, however, more than poverty, is the primary facet of otherness in prison narratives, and therefore minority positions based on race, interracial relations, and racism are central to my study. Scholars such as Marc Mauer and Angela Davis, for example, claim that race—and blackness, in particular—has become normalized as a defining factor of criminality in the United States.[19] This, these scholars assert, is the effect of embedded racism in the criminal justice system, and in the consequent assumptions about who the criminals are in U.S. society. Racial disparities are obvious in current incarceration rates. Approximately 50 percent of all U.S. inmates are African American, compared to their 13 percent share of the overall population; 32 percent of black males aged 20 to 29 are under criminal justice supervision; 7 percent of adult black males and 1 percent of white males were in prison in 1995; a black male born in 1991 has a 29 percent chance of spending time in prison at some point in his life—the figure for Latinos is 16 percent and, for whites, 4 percent.[20] The racial disparity in incarceration rates reworks and complicates the relationships between minority-majority positions in U.S. prisons; what is socially considered a "minority" often becomes a "majority" in the context of prison narratives.

When discussing race, I approach the concept as a discursive system of representation that reflects the ideology of race in the United States—stereotypic representations of minorities as the other and white supremacy, for example. Since these concepts and their representations are deeply rooted in socio-historical fact, I situate my analysis in a specific social and historical setting and consider the concept of race also to be a "subject of political contestation" (Omi vii). Therefore, I do not treat contemporary prison narratives *only* as representations of life in prison, but also as a window through which aspects of the discourses of race, gender, and sexuality in the post-civil rights era United States in general can be understood. From this point of view, the changing minority-majority positions in the social context of prisons provides a model for analyzing a phenomenon that is becoming or has already become an actuality in the United States in cities like Los Angeles, for instance, where whites are no longer a racial majority.

The pattern of racial representation that most readily emerges in prison narratives is the black-white dynamic,[21] and therefore my study necessarily reflects the notion of black and white as racial polar opposites—a way of thinking that is outdated in contemporary discourses of race. This is not to say that contemporary prison narratives merely represent a stagnant manner of representing race, but, on the contrary, the resistance mode that I trace in my study also appears in the context of rethinking the concept of race and interracial relationships. However, prison narratives do rely on traditional ways of looking at race in terms of blackness against whiteness, and vice versa, and express the ideology of transparency of race that holds that white is the unmarked racial category and that "race" only applies as a minority marker.

Since race and masculinity are my primary concerns, these topics interact and overlap with each other throughout my discussion. Chapters One, Two, and Three are structured around specific subgenres of prison narratives—science fiction film, autobiography, and the novel—and Chapter Four brings all the different strands of otherness together to take a more holistic view of prison narratives under the theme of surveillance. By studying contemporary prison narratives in both ways, subgenre by subgenre and as a whole, I point out what is most typical to each subgenre and also delineate the prison narrative as a genre that deserves critical attention.

Since most prisoners are men, narratives representing life in prison are, to a great extent, projections of masculinity and male subjectivity. As masculinist narratives, prison narratives display the kinds of tales of violence, endurance, and heroic deeds that are typical of male subjectivity in American culture. James Baldwin has pointed out that what violence and heroism are typical of, in particular, in American society is *white* masculinity. He writes that, "[I]n the United States, violence and heroism have been made synonymous except when it comes to blacks," and the "real reason that non-violence is considered to be a virtue in Negroes . . . is that white men do not want their lives, their self-image, or their property threatened" (68, 69).

In Chapter One, "The Future of Imprisonment: Contemporary Science Fiction and Documentary Film," I analyze how two futuristic "escape from" prison films—Stuart Gordon's *Fortress* (1993) and Martin Campbell's *No Escape* (1994)—envision the future of imprisonment as globally managed businesses. Although these films extrapolate incarceration as a continuation of today's privatization trend and express a dark view of the dehumanizing effects imprisonment has on both inmates and the prison management, the representations of raced masculinities in the films retain traditional ideas of white male supremacy reaching new frontiers, while non-white male characters are left behind or die trying to escape. I argue that, while science fiction films are progressive in their critique of the current ideologies of imprisonment and in their representation of homoerotic tension in prison sexuality, they remain conservative in their treatment of the issues of race and gender. In this chapter I also discuss documentaries that present a dystopic view of incarceration—today and tomorrow—with a focus on the dangers of the modern high-tech "lock 'em up and throw away the key" mentality.

In Chapter Two, "African American Prison Autobiography: From Racial to Sexual Politics," I focus on the specific nature of prison sexuality and examine how it is crucial to the representations of black masculinity and interracial relationships in a homosocial environment. Historically, African American manhood has been represented as primarily corporeal, exotic, and eroticized—and as such—dangerous. From D. W. Griffith's *The Birth of a Nation,* filmic representations of black masculinity, in particular, have focused on the black male body as dangerously sexual.[23] Since black men are also seen as the archetypal criminals in American society, African American prison autobiographers face the task of redefining black manhood against these cultural and social assumptions while simultaneously retaining what appears positive in representations of black male sexual prowess.

Since popular prison narratives constantly foreground homosexuality and male-male rape, prison autobiographers must address these issues as well. Autobiographical work typically negates homosexuality by structuring same-sex relationships as temporary behavior rather than as an essential part of the prisoner's sexual identity. African American autobiographers tend to assert their heterosexuality by detaching themselves from the male-male sexual situations. I argue that, in so doing, the authors demonstrate that male-male sexual acts in prison in fact shape the sexual identity of the prisoners, and do not merely function as ways of asserting power relations or as outlets for race-related anger. To consider my argument from a different perspective, I examine Tomás Almaguer's "Chicano Men: A Cartography of Homosexual Identity and Behavior" (1993), in which he claims that Chicano homosexual identity is structured along the axis of dominance and submissiveness, where the "active" participant of the act is not considered homosexual, while the "passive" participant is. Therefore, homosexual identity itself is defined by power relations rather than by object choice.

Drawing on Linda Singer's *Erotic Welfare: Sexual Theory and Politics in the Age of Epidemic* (1993) I also discuss how the institutional practices that are meant to regulate same-sex relations actually produce sexual acts, both in a discursive manner and as actual experiences. Thus, the homophobic ideology that aims at controlling sexuality in prisons generates prison sex as a representational fetish and, at the same time, accepts male-male rape as *the* form of homosexual intercourse in the context of prison.

In Chapter Three, "Divide and Conquer: Racialized Hierarchies in the Contemporary Prison Novel," I analyze how the ideology of racial difference is reflected in and shapes the logic of imprisonment by taking a look at race-based social hierarchies in prison. By primarily focusing on Nathan C. Heard's novel *House of Slammers* (1983), I argue that the racial hierarchies that seem normalized in prison narratives are, to a large extent, created by the institution of prison and by the subtle racism within its practices of classifying prisoners.

In this chapter I also discuss James Edward Olmos' *American Me* (1992) and Taylor Hackford's *Blood In, Blood Out* (1993), films that explore Latino experience and agency with a focus on prison gangs and their broader influence on Los Angeles communities. I analyze the role of prison gangs within the context of Michael Omi and Howard Winant's notion of race as a "social structure and cultural representation," and as a "sociohistorical process" based on historical conflict and the discursive crisis of racial representation related to it (56, 55, 60–61).

In Chapter Four, "Surveillance and Prisoner Identity: Imprisoned Bodies as the American Other," I bring the various subgenres of prison narratives together in order to demonstrate how surveillance—or being constantly watched in a manifold of ways—structures the identity of the prisoner as the American cultural, social, and national "other." I apply Stephen Paul Miller's notion that "cultural self-surveillance" is enabled by social, ideological, and discursive "identity prisms" that reinforce individual identification (19) to argue that the prisoner subjectivity is constructed, in part, with the public image of the criminal as a panoptic disciplinary model, and also as the focal point of resistance. Thus the monitoring proper, performed by the penal institution, is doubled by the image of the criminal in the visual media. In the context of surveillance, I also analyze how masculinity—and femininity as part of prison masculinity—are structured through the male gaze on a male body.

"Epilogue: Global Effects of U.S. Discourses of Imprisonment" focuses on critiques of the potential global effect of U.S. penal policies that are "the harshest in American history and of any Western country" (Tonry, "Crime" 3). Although the self-appointed position of the United States as the world-disciplinarian has traditionally been strongly criticized by other countries, criminologists argue that its current position as the only superpower gives its penal policies global political significance. In this context I also address how the cultural discursive ideologies of incarceration and criminality in the U.S. permeate national cultural discourses globally as they are introduced by the media and popular culture and then recirculated as normalized in cultural contexts that are alien to them.

My study demonstrates how racism and homophobia, in particular, figure in the constitution and revision of criminal male identities in contemporary American prison narratives. It has special urgency at a historical moment in the "war on crime" when the crime rates are at record low, yet incarceration rates are growing rapidly.[23] Currently, because states spend more on prisons than on higher education, in effect prisons "have become our nation's substitute for effective public policies on crime, drugs, mental illness, housing, poverty, and employment of the hardest-to-employ."[24] My study of prison narratives shows that, at this time, the political function of the prison is more central than its penal function and that the image of the criminal serves *symbolic* social and cultural needs more than it illustrates the purposes and goals of the criminal justice system in the United States.

Chapter One

The Future of Imprisonment: Contemporary Science Fiction and Documentary Film

Fredric Jameson has claimed that the genre of science fiction evolved because of the difficulty of dealing with the present. As a medium for understanding the present, science fiction has replaced the historical novel: the present that was perceived to be a consequence of historical events is now conceived as the past of something that will happen in the future. Jameson writes that, rather than "seriously attempt[ing] to imagine the 'real' future of our social system," works of science fiction have the "function of transforming our own present into the determinate past of something yet to come" (152). Since the present is culturally "inaccessible directly" to us, science fiction "enacts and enables a structurally unique 'method' for apprehending the present as history" (151, 153). Thus, the primary function of science fiction is "not to give us 'images' of the future," but "to defamiliarize and restructure our experience of our own *present*" (151).

Perhaps this kind of cultural inability or social reluctance to see the present U.S. criminal justice system as it is explains the apparent temporal and spatial displacement of narratives of imprisonment in contemporary prison films. Within the discursive system of "historical novel to science fiction" that Jameson outlines, contemporary prison films fall into two major categories: historical films that defamiliarize and restructure prison experience through romanticizing it, or science fiction films that defamiliarize and restructure prison experience through demonizing prisons of the future.

Historical films such as *The Shawshank Redemption* (1994), *The Green Mile* (1999), and *O Brother, Where Art Thou?* (2000) fantasize imprisonment and the escape from it by depicting the main characters as fallible, but innocent of any serious crime, and by locating prison experience in the romantic American countryside of the past. *O Brother, Where Art Thou?*, with its soundtrack expressing the sensibilities of hillbilly culture, in particular, appeals to the sense of the innocence and simplicity of the past of an American life untainted by criminality.

Science fiction films, on the other hand, locate prisons on remote islands and in a distant future that simultaneously represents the "determinate past" of the future corrections system of the United States. The films that are the main focus in this chapter, Martin Campbell's *No Escape* (1994) and Stuart Gordon's *Fortress* (1993), create the present of U.S. criminal justice system by imagining it in the future.[1] These films defamiliarize the current trends in imprisonment—such as the privatization of prisons, the implementation of longer mandatory or indeterminate sentencing,[2] and the ongoing debate on the penal viability and moral justifiability of the death penalty, for instance—by locating them in the past of future times.

In this chapter I discuss futuristic prison films as the genre of the late 20th century that both reflects the growing public anxiety about the prison industrial complex and criticizes the American criminal justice system for its inhumane treatment of prisoners in modern, high-tech maximum security prisons. I argue that the prison film is the genre that, to a great extent, filled the void created by the repression of prison literature during the 1980s and 1990s discussed by H. Bruce Franklin in *Prison Writing in 20th-Century America*. The prison film, I argue, counteracts the legal measures that regulate prisoner writing and "keep American people in the dark about the American prison" (Franklin 14). Because of the lack of regulation of the production of prison-related feature films and because of the popularity of crime-based action movies, filmmakers are in the opportune position to explore current public concerns about the escalation of imprisonment and the consequent criminalization of large sections of the population.

As futuristic texts, *No Escape* and *Fortress* also reflect issues typical of science fiction by examining the human desire for testing the limits of humanity and, more importantly, the consequent fear of change, the fear of breaching the boundaries between man and machine. In these films, the fear of machines—or cyborg-like beings—taking over the management of prisons in the future is resolved through the return to the primitive. The return to the primitive—in addition to implicating a clear-cut difference between man and machine—also expresses nostalgia for the times when the difference between traditional male and female spheres of action seemed obvious. In these films, the man kills in order to escape the evil machine-governed world and the woman gives birth; and, from the moment of the escape, the fear of the invisible, unnatural, and technological is assuaged by the safety of the visible, natural, and biological.

Futuristic prison movies also focus on the fear of change in the concept of crime itself. Crime is no longer something "outside" of organized society, but instead is within the system of society itself, where the government or its justice system is the criminal and the citizens its innocent victims. In *No Escape,* the "crime" of the protagonist is his opposition to corrupt authority, a theme shared with several other films of this genre. In *Fortress,* reproduction has been criminalized in the United States: only one child per woman is allowed, even if that child dies. Crimes such as these that are political rather than violent in nature suggest a new generation of political prisoners, the existence of which has traditionally been denied by the U.S. criminal justice system.[3]

The international maximum-security prisons in these two movies also represent the current fear that in the era of global policing—enabled by sophisticated surveillance systems—the humanness of incarcerated individuals will be annihilated by technology run amok or by the corporate mad scientists controlling it. The politicization of what constitutes crime in the future U.S. criminal justice system, combined with the fact that crime management has been passed over to global corporations, further intensifies the fear that the future criminal justice system will be devoid of justice; privately owned imprisoned human bodies will have no chance for appeal or pardon in the future global economy.

Yet, because of the change in the concept of crime, these films do not take a stand against the imprisonment of criminals who commit crimes that are typical in today's society—violent crimes and drug-related crimes, for example.[4] It is striking, however, that the prisoners whose crimes are clearly more political in nature—such as a breach with government authority—are white and "innocent," while prisoners convicted of more traditional crimes are depicted as non-white and "guilty." Within the escape-from films (the main genre of prison films), the white and innocent man escapes while the guilty non-white man is left behind or is eradicated during his attempt to escape. This tendency to racialize guilt and innocence reaffirms the current notion in U.S. society that African American and Latino males are criminals.

Besides this tendency to racialize criminal behavior, futuristic prison movies also tend to perpetuate what Kaja Silverman calls the "dominant fiction": the (patriarchal) ideology of the stability of heterosexuality and family (15–16). Although these films may create homoerotic tension between male characters, and by doing so suggest a possibility of homosexual relationships between them, the tension is repudiated through measures that reaffirm the systems of heterosexuality and male dominance.

A major focus of this chapter is the manner in which the American male survives his test of masculinity in the prison of the future. For a man, imprisonment—being prohibited from moving and being constantly acted upon—not only signifies the loss of his humanness, but also the deprivation of his masculinity. To retain masculinity, the prison reform that some recent futuristic movies suggest projects prisons as communities in which inmates actively participate in running the prisons. In other words, the men in prison are transformed from objects to subjects. In terms of retaining phallic masculinity, prison films also suggest some paradoxical differences between problems in correctional institutions of the present and the future. For example, although contemporary prisons reduce human contact to an absolute minimum and their wardens express concern about the over-crowding of their geriatric wards, futuristic movies focus on coed prisons[5] and the question of procreation.

If we consider products of popular culture as radically resisting established social and cultural beliefs, recent futuristic American prison movies do just that—they display a strong cultural angst about the presumption that incarceration is an answer to all social ills in the United States. While the current "tough-on-crime" public opinion is highly pro-imprisonment, prison movies problematize incarceration and challenge its feasibility as a solution to crime management in the future. Filmmakers as well as criminologists are concerned about the legitimacy and value of prison sentences as such and about the inhumane conditions to which prisoners are subjected by "post-correction age" maximum-security prisons, a reality in the United States since the early 1980s.

From another perspective, because futuristic prison films such as *No Escape* and *Fortress* fail to imagine changes in race and gender relations—and therefore persist in traditional racist and sexist representations—they resist the postmodernist mode of examining the complexity of concepts and values. When addressing the issue of guilt and innocence, these films suggest that prisoners can be guilty and innocent at the same time, depending on the specific nature of their crimes. Thus they re-evaluate and broaden the concepts and value systems concerning criminality, but not of those concerning race and gender.

To discuss the contrasts between fictive visions of incarcerated masculinity and those indicated by the real-life conditions of contemporary U.S. prisons, I examine two documentary films, "Crime and Punishment" and *The Farm: Life Inside Angola Prison*. A major difference between the genres representing the future of imprisonment—the documentary and the science fiction film—is the manner in which they focus on the incarcerated male individual. The documentaries primarily represent the prisoner as a victim of the penal code or of the criminal justice system in general. The futuristic prison films, on the other hand, represent prisoners as heroes resisting their treatment as Foucaultian "docile bodies," and propose an incarcerated subjectivity that can and will resist the totalizing and individualizing power of the system.

Ted Koppel's serial documentary produced for ABC television, "Crime and Punishment" (1998), paints a bleak picture of the present condition of U.S. prisons and projects a future where the men who have survived incarceration in a maximum security prison constitute an inevitable threat "on the streets" of tomorrow's America. Koppel characterizes contemporary American "supermax" prisons as "monuments of failure" because of their inability to offer any hope for those individuals who go through the system, and therefore seems to be sympathetic with the prisoners' view of imprisonment as a needlessly dehumanizing experience. The documentary series nevertheless feeds the paranoia and fear of crime and criminals by depicting these men as already psychotic and thus as unavoidable threats to future society.

The Farm: Life Inside Angola Prison (1998)—directed by Jonathan Stack and Liz Garbus and co-directed by Wilbert Rideau, an inmate at the Louisiana State Penitentiary in Angola—also assumes the point of view of the individual prisoner. Unlike the sensationalizing stance of Koppel's documentary, *The Farm* presents inmates as ordinary people with feelings and aspirations and focuses on the prison population as a community in its own right, not merely through its relationship to the society outside the prison walls. Because most inmates in Angola face a future with no parole (Warden Cain states that 85 percent of Angola's inmates never return to society), the major problem of the facility is its growing number of elderly or terminally ill prisoners. In fact, the film opens and closes with a scene of a funeral of an inmate who was buried at the prison cemetery.

The dystopic vision of the future of the prison industry, and of the U.S. criminal justice system in general, that recent futuristic prison films project is reflective of the present "tough-on-crime" ideology and the consequent expansion of mandatory sentencing that has created a vastly growing number of new "criminals." Constance Penley defines movies which "point to present tendencies that seem likely to result in corporate totalitarianism, apocalypse, or both" as *critical dystopias* (63). According to Penley, critical dystopias "[locate] the origins of future catastrophe in decisions about technology . . . and social behavior that are being made today" (63). With their focus on the inhumane conditions of maximum security prisons, the criminalization of natural human behavior such as procreation, and the creation of a criminal underclass to serve as slave-like subjects for a privately-owned prison industry, futuristic prison films function as critical dystopias. The present tendencies that seem likely to result in future catastrophes (extrapolated in these films) already exist in the U.S. criminal justice system: the conditions in some maximum security prisons have received severe criticism, pregnant women have been imprisoned until the birth of their babies because their lifestyles allegedly put the lives of their unborn babies in danger, and the privatization and industrialization of prisons (with prisoners as an extremely low-paid and captive workforce) is expanding rapidly.

Although they express a critical view of the prison system, science fiction films retain racist, sexist, and homophobic ideas about prisoner identity. As Stuart Hall has pointed out, this seeming contradiction of aims is typical of pop culture. He writes, "we should always start . . . with the double-stake in popular culture, the double movement of containment and resistance, which is always inevitably inside it" (228). In futuristic prison films, this double movement of containment and resistance is visible in the manner in which the radical critique of the institution of prison and the criminal justice system at large is coupled with traditional views about how the problems of the future global prison industrial complex can be resolved. The political and ethical issues raised by these films are resolved when the traditional American white male hero enacts the national fantasy of an escape to a new frontier, whether the new frontier is primitive Mexico in *Fortress* or, more metaphorically, a brighter future after the systemic injustices have been made public by the worldwide media in *No Escape*.

Fortress and *No Escape* thus negotiate the modes of resistance and containment in ways that are typical of products of popular culture. As critical dystopias, these movies voice concerns about the changes in the criminal justice system that the ideologies of the globalized corporate prison industry may create, but simultaneously they contain such persistent and racialized cultural fantasies as the American (white male) innocence on a quest to save the world, and reinforce the stability of systems of heterosexuality and male dominance. Thus, these movies are politically ambivalent—simultaneously radical and conservative. The future crime management envisioned by these films reflects concerns about global (and totalitarian) corporate economies and the highly technological or primitive systems of crime management in the future United States. Both issues, the globalized criminal justice system and the issue of either high-tech or primitive solutions to crime management, are responses to a future society that has radically disintegrated, usually in the aftermath of a nuclear disaster, and evolved into a totalitarian state in which the concept of crime has been politicized and the ownership of political prisoners has been given over to corporations. These corporations commodify and utilize the prison population in ways that negate the prisoners' human rights.

The link between modern capitalism and the prison institution that science fiction prison films explore is outlined in Michel Foucault's *Discipline and Punish: The Birth of the Prison* (1975). According to Foucault, "a capitalist economy gave rise to [a] specific modality of disciplinary power," which both economically and politically facilitated the "accumulation of men" (220–221). The accumulation of men further enhanced the accumulation of capital (221). These basic circumstances—the accumulation of men and capital—together with the disciplinary "technology of subjection" based on military models made it possible for prisons to function as industrial enterprises in the late 18ᵗʰ century (221). Therefore, capital economy and prisons as industry can be seen as mutually dependent. The view that prisons, as industrial enterprises, are to be managed in the most economic way possible has been adopted by penal decision makers in the present-day United States as well, and thus privately owned companies and global corporations are seen as lucrative solutions for raising the productivity of prisons as businesses.[6]

While the productivity of prisons managed as businesses may be high, the interests of private owners obviously clash with penal interests and with the interests of taxpayers and prisoners. As Vivian Stern notes, a host of industries thrives on the needs of the imprisoned: builders and designers of prisons, sellers and buyers of various prison equipment, workers to "guard, feed, clothe, educate, provide telephones" for people in prisons, and specialists to subject prisoners to "psychological testing and urine sampling" (289). The circumstances of modern incarceration seem to speak to the validity of Foucault's assertion that the accumulation of men—or prisoners—facilitates the accumulation of capital, which in turn facilitates accumulation of more men, because the capital has been used to build more prisons to contain them. Considering the penal interest, though, Stern argues that mass incarceration is the "least effective way of reducing crime" because it is expensive, people do not feel any safer, and prisoners are unnecessarily imprisoned "well beyond their crime-prone years" (289). Thus, in privatized and globalized prison management "tax-payer money" is used to line the pockets of private business owners, while at the same time crime is not reduced.

Although prisons in contemporary futuristic prison films still lie within the geographic and cultural space of the United States—the locations are in the United States, the value systems are unmistakably American, and most characters speak in the same American English accent[7]—these prisons are global in the sense that they represent the globalization of capital and the ownership of prisoners in a global economy. Therefore, although the films assert that the problems in the prison industry are caused by its privatization and globalization, they clearly focus on imprisonment as a local concern, and thus project the future history of American incarceration. The premises of these films seem to parallel those of Michel Foucault; the existence of prisons as industrial, profitable institutions and the disciplinary technologies of subjection they employ are directly linked to the practices of capitalism, and in the future, to post-industrial global capitalism in particular. Besides extrapolating a world economy where people can be owned as a workforce, where prisoners are colonial-like subjects of international correctional institutions, contemporary futuristic prison movies also examine the effects of such globalizing systems as electronic control devices that make any human contact between the prisoners and their guards unnecessary.

Stuart Gordon's 1993 film *Fortress* opens with features characteristic of both prison films and science fiction films. The heavily armed guards at a U.S. Border Station watch over when John and Karen Brennick (Christopher Lambert and Loryn Locklin) go through a security point and have the barcode IDs tattooed on their forearms bio-scanned by a border security officer. In rapid sequence of scenes, Karen Brennick is caught wearing a vest that hides her pregnancy and escapes, and John Brennick, after being seized by guard dogs, is arrested. His crime: attempting to take his wife to give birth to their second child abroad because having multiple children has been criminalized in the United States. His sentence: 31 years. In the following scenes, the camera pans a desert with a vehicle—which turns out to be the transportation to the correctional facility—driving by. From the outside, the vehicle looks like a garbage truck and, from the inside, it resembles the railway cars used to transport Jews to concentration camps during the Holocaust. The scene economically expresses the association of human prisoners, fittingly squeezed together in a small space and dressed in rags, as garbage being disposed of.

The initiation ritual for Brennick and other criminals of the future consists of the traditional strip search scene, while the voice and televised picture of prison Director Poe (Kurtwood Smith) greets the inmates with, "everything here is the property of MEN-TEL Corporation—including you."[8] Director Poe also informs incoming prisoners that the Federal Government pays the Corporation $27 per day per prisoner, work shifts run 24 hours per day, and, in addition to their physical movements, prisoners' thoughts are also monitored. The initiation scene is completed by prisoners being outfitted with an "intestinator"—a metal "behavior control device" that facilitates their monitoring. The intestinators are shot inside the prisoners' bodies through their mouths with a phallic instrument, simulating a forced oral intercourse. The symbolic rape scene foreshadows the actual rape scene later in the film, a scene that is part of the discursive core of treatments of sexuality in prison narratives in general. Also, the voice-over that repeats the slogan, "Crime does not pay," seems to refer to the commonly, if not openly, accepted thought that the institutionalized emasculation and rape of the male prisoners is part of the punishment.

The surveillance system of the prison that Brennick enters is like a Bentham's Panopticon for the computer age. The section of the building where the prisoners are kept consists of a central unit with tiers of cells surrounding it; the tiers divide prisoners according to gender and criminal status. The sophisticated surveillance system of the facility does not only "make it possible to see constantly and to recognize immediately," but also includes an electronic component, Zed-10 (with a sensuous female voice-over), that enables the observation and control of the prisoners' thoughts (Foucault, *Discipline and Punish* 200). The prisoners' thoughts are also deemed so dangerous to the system that they are censored. Brennick gets his first punishment in the facility for dreaming about having sex with his wife; simultaneously Director Poe gets voyeuristic pleasure from viewing Brennick's dreams on a multi-screen video system. The ubiquitous computer presence, Zed-10, also controls the controller, Director Poe, ensuring that "power is not totally entrusted to someone who would exercise it alone, over others, in an absolute fashion" (Foucault, "The Eye of Power" 156). This system of apparently multiple and unsubstantial sources for control creates a sense of paranoia in the prisoners and therein translates into self-monitoring surveillance in a Panoptic manner.

The opening of Martin Campbell's *No Escape* (1994) also speaks about absolute control and the surveillance of prisoners. The first aerial shot shows columns of marching correctional officers in guerilla war-like uniforms casually performing the execution of an unidentified prisoner. The scene is reminiscent of Fritz Lang's classic science fiction film *Metropolis* (1926), which predicted the adverse consequences of the totalitarian Nazi regime and the industrial revolution. The score offers a stark contrast to the dark mood of the scene, which is emphasized by the various shades-of-gray coloring of the prison interior: the tune on the soundtrack, with its merry piccolos and perky drums, is similar to the jolly rhythms of "Yankee Doodle." The musical element, then, reminds us of a war fought on American soil.

The scenes that follow introduce the film's protagonist, ex-Special Forces commander John Robbins (Ray Liotta), and the Warden (Michael Lerner), who first appears to the prisoners as a floating, incorporeal blue blob. The scene cuts to the Warden's office where he studies a computer file of Robbins that shows a DNA-scan revealing his crime to be his "pathological aversion to authority" (even though he was convicted of murdering his commanding officer, a war crime). The Warden, like Director Poe, introduces his facility as a "multi-national business" that stores "garbage from around the world"—men for whom "society has no further use." Robbins is told that there will be no contact with the world outside; in practical terms the prisoners have ceased to exist. As the final stage of his punishment, Robbins is flown to an island serving as a secret depository for dangerous criminals who are monitored by a spy satellite. The island community, Absolom, consists of two warring groups of criminals, both living in primitive *Robinson Crusoe* or *Cast Away*-like conditions.

Both *No Escape* and *Fortress* foreground the fear that changes in the concept of crime spawn. The crimes in the future are political, in the sense that the public does not accept them as crimes, and also invisible, in the sense that the real crimes are committed inside the prisons by the institutions themselves, approved by a government that is supposed to protect its citizens against such criminal activity. In *Fortress,* the law criminalizing a woman "breeding," or having a second child, was passed as a solution for world hunger. In contrast to childless couples, MEN-TEL Corporation can claim ownership of all babies born in its facility. These babies are used for human "enhancement"—for creating cyborgs that have little need for nutrition or sleep, and that are unable to copulate, and therefore to procreate. The director of the correctional facility is one of the enhanced human beings owned by MEN-TEL. The Corporation also produces and utilizes cyborgs whose major prosthetic device is the human brain. The future that this film suggests, then, is of diminishing numbers of humans and increasing numbers of cyborgs with considerably longer life spans than humans.

John Robbins, in *No Escape,* is convicted of murder, but through a series of flashbacks viewers learn that he killed his commanding officer because that officer was guilty of a war crime. By killing him, Robbins becomes an accomplice to a government cover-up, and must therefore be imprisoned. Robbins' nightmarish flashbacks to the war crime repeat a scene reminiscent of the My Lai massacre in which women and children flee a flaming village. The commanding officer's crime was far more serious than Robbins'—and the officer seems to have deserved his death sentence—yet it is Robbins, an individual refusing to comply with corruption, who is punished. His mission, besides exposing the secret island penitentiary to the world, is also to find personal vindication for being convicted of a crime of which he, from an ethical point of view, is innocent.

The protagonists of *No Escape* and *Fortress* are innocent in the sense that the current popular sense of what is criminal would not define them as responsible for the crimes of which they were convicted. Therefore, these movies imply that if the present legislative tendencies in criminal law continue—implementing mandatory prison sentences, the "three-strikes" laws, for example—future prisons will be filled with people who the public deems innocent. The prisoners are also represented as victims of invisible crimes in a system perpetuated by their fellow prisoners, who are also their keepers. The correctional systems of the future depicted in these films rob prisoners of their citizenship and their human subjectivity. The fact that prisoners exist in slave-like conditions is kept a secret from the national and international communities because neither would accept this.[9]

The themes of war, military-style totalitarian prison systems, and secrecy surrounding cancelled citizenships and violated human rights allegorize both the ideologies of the Cold War and the current "war on crime." Vivian Stern argues that the contemporary war ethos is carried over from the times of the Cold War: today, however, the "prison world is a battleground. The prisoners are the enemy . . . A whole sector of US industry is now devoted to the war against US citizens" (303).[10] Criminologist Nils Christie also notes that, since most major industrial nations have no external enemies, it seems probable that "the war against the inner enemies will receive top priority" (16). This sentiment is apparent in futuristic prison movies as well. Prisoners are morally and ethically innocent of the crimes of which they are accused, yet are treated as the expendable enemy of correctional institutions that are constantly developing new proactive defense mechanisms, primarily surveillance systems, that make human contact obsolete. The experiments forced on prisoners—the "mind wipe chamber" and the "enhancement" of babies in *Fortress,* and the testing the prisoners' survival skills in a civil war jungle in *No Escape,* for example—also suggest how the U.S. government uses its citizens as guinea pigs for future wars. Thus, the films seem to support Christie's argument that "[t]he major dangers of crime in modern societies are not the crimes, but that the fight against them may lead societies toward totalitarian developments" (16).

The "escape-from" filmic imagery, however, creates a revolutionary subject—the non-compromising all-American hero—who epitomizes the importance of rebelling against government ordained authority. Invariably, it is the *white* male, the rebel with an aversion for authority, who escapes. In *Fortress*, Brennick escapes with his pregnant wife to start a new life in Mexico; in *No Escape*, Robbins escapes to reveal the secrets of the corrupt prison system and the military operation related to it, while Hawkins (Ernie Hudson), the only African American male with a speaking role in the film, stays behind to manage the island penitentiary.[11]

In fact, the white male protagonist appears as the natural leader from the very moment he enters the prison facility and he typically displays his hero-worth and aggressive masculinity by fighting a fellow inmate. In *Fortress*, Brennick first defends himself against the sexual advances of his cellmate, Stiggs (Tom Towles), and then fights Stiggs' friend, Maddox (Vernon Wells), a murderous giant who sexually assaulted another cellmate, the Latino Nino (Clifton Gonzáles Gonzáles). In the aftermath of another fight with Maddox, Brennick is ordered to kill him, but he again challenges authority by refusing to do so. In *No Escape*, Robbins kills the bodyguard of the self-appointed leader of the "Outsiders," Marek (Stuart Wilson), and then defeats Marek himself by tricking him off his machine gun—a highly phallic black weapon and the only one on the island—and thus proving his superior masculinity.

The prison community of Absolom is divided into two warring groups, the "Insiders" and the "Outsiders." The Insiders are an organized, civilized community of 97 men, led by Father (Lance Henriksen), while the Outsiders are a cruel mob-oriented community of about 600 savages. In addition to these differences, Insiders and Outsiders differ from each other in a distinctly racialized manner. Almost all Insiders appear white—with the notable exception of the African American Chief of Security, Hawkins, whose rippling muscles are revealed by his skimpy tank top. While Insiders are white, the Outsiders are savages in black face with blackened bodies. They wear masks and loincloth, are armed with primitive spears and slings, sound much like "Indians" in American Westerns or the hoards of identity-less "savages" in classic Tarzan movies, and are appropriately accompanied by drumming on the soundtrack. Therefore, the Insiders represent the white and the civilized (they wear ordinary Western clothes, shave their faces, and read books) while the Outsiders represent the dark and the savage. The hero, Robbins, with his smooth face, clear blue eyes, neat haircut, and clean clothes, forms a stark contrast to the bearded, dark Marek and his primitive mob.

The protagonists, who are criminally averse to governmental authority, often also represent it. Robbins had a military career and Brennick is said to be the "most decorated Captain in the history of the Black Beret," although he "quit in disgrace" because, according to his prison file, he "lost an entire platoon." The tendency to cast the protagonists as ex-members of the military (or the police force) [12] may be indicative of the contemporary distrust of these institutions, but it also gives the protagonists a certain kind of plausibility and agency. The expectations for the genre of "escape-from" action movie seem to require a hero-leader who is able and trained to physically remove obstacles in close combat and, when necessary, kill enemies as a reflex-like response. Characters like Andy Dufresne in *The Shawshank Redemption* who can beat the system purely with their intellect are very rare. The fact that the protagonists represent the authority also signifies that, although the institutions in general may be corrupt, there are heroic individuals who—with their vigilante tactics—can make a positive difference within these institutions.

The white male protagonists thus represent innocence in contemporary futuristic prison films, and interestingly, it is their *crimes* that make them innocent. Robbins may have murdered his commanding officer, but since the murder was a punishment for the officer's culpability for killing women and children, Robbins' crime is justified. Brennick likewise breaks the law by fathering a second child, but that crime is also not deemed criminal in the film. Robbins and Brennick, then, despite their status as criminals, are represented as morally superior to the authorities that criminalize them. Since the escaping protagonists are in most cases white, the concept of crime also becomes racialized. We do not know the crimes of which the very few African American or Latino prisoners in these films were convicted, but these prisoners clearly do not occupy the position of righteous rebels against a corrupt system. Interestingly, the authority figures against which the white protagonists fight are also represented by white actors. The whiteness of the authority is highlighted by recurring references to totalitarian ideologies like fascism and slavery that advocate the superiority of the white race.

The most striking comparison of a prisoner to a slave occurs in *Fortress,* in which the character of Abraham, an African American prisoner, is portrayed in a slave-like position. Abraham—who typically for slaves or servants, does not seem to have a last name—is Director Poe's valet and it is implied that Poe, despite the letters to the parole board he is supposedly writing, is determined never to let him go. In his interaction with Poe, Abraham is highly submissive, which is illustrated by his downcast eyes and his air of not seeing, not hearing, and not speaking. It seems that, in American prison films, the only chance for a black male to exit a prison before he has completed his sentence is under the supervision of a white police officer, as in *48 Hrs.* (1982), where Reggie Hammond (Eddie Murphy) is released for 48 hours to help Officer Jack Cates (Nick Nolte) catch the criminals who killed his colleagues.

The idea of the escape—instigated by the traditional American white hero—as a viable solution to the political and ethical issues that contemporary futuristic prison movies pose points to two clusters of interpretive options. First, the modern utopian belief in individual human agency seems to represent the "containment" part of the "double-stake" in popular culture, as opposed to the "resistance" these movies offer to the notion that mass imprisonment will solve all societal problems in the United States (Hall 228).

On the other hand, the manner in which prisoners are characterized as heroes "promot[es] new forms of subjectivity" for imprisoned individuals (Foucault, "The Subject and Power" 216). Michel Foucault places the promotion of new forms of subjectivity in "The Subject and Power," in the context of what he calls the "most certain" of current philosophical problems—the "problem of the present time" and the problem of "what we are" (216). He suggests that the question of what we are today is "[m]aybe . . . not to discover what we are, but to *refuse* what we are" (216, my italics). In our quest to refuse what we are, according to Foucault, we resist the "simultaneous individualization and totalization of modern power structures" in order to "liberate us both from the state and from the type of individualization which is linked to the state" (216). Foucault's hypothesis applies to the kind of "liberation" process evident in futuristic prison films. I argue that by transgressing the current popular images of prisoners being "garbage" or "non-human," and by depicting characters who actively resist the workings of the Foucaultian techniques of individualizing and totalizing power, these films promote new prison subjectivities.

No Escape and *Fortress* suggest that there is no single source for power in the U.S.-based crime management of the future. References to the global and international ownership of prisons and prisoners combined with the local management run by the mad-scientist warden in *No Escape*, and by the team of the cyborg-Director Poe and Zed-10 computer in *Fortress* create a complex sense of the distribution of power. The computerized data-collecting and surveillance mechanisms form a centralized system that has the ability to exercise the kind of power that makes each prisoner "a describable, analysable object . . . under the gaze of a permanent corpus of knowledge" (Foucault, *Discipline and Punish* 190). This kind of totalizing effect is apparent in the way that the prisoners are turned into "disciplinary objects" by individualizing means that are used to classify, manipulate, and control them. In Foucault's words, the use of the individualizing technologies "makes each individual a 'case' . . . that constitutes an object for a branch of knowledge and a hold for a branch of power" (191).

In both *No Escape* and *Fortress*, prisoners' bodies are objectified in a manner that justifies the human fear of the loss of subjectivity, a concern often expressed in works of science fiction. The prisoners' individual identities are turned into numbers, digital bar codes, and classifications according to criminal types. Their bodies are also drafted to build new prison facilities, treated as renewable human resources for "enhancement" as prosthetic devices for constructing cyborgs, and used as material for disciplinary spectacles. Also, their minds are controlled through surveillance of their thoughts and dreams, which in turn function as spectacular pleasures for their keepers. The human bodies and minds of the prisoners are being constantly looked at and looked into, and thus treated like objects or test animals from which the "state" can learn how to make other human bodies into more easily treatable prisoners.

By refusing to be treated as objects and to become "subjectified"—that is, refusing to turn themselves into passive "subjects" (to use Foucault's terminology)—the white male heroes of futuristic prison films promote new forms of prisoner subjectivity. Instead of submitting to the individualizing and totalizing powers of the U.S. criminal justice system that the "state" exerts upon them, the protagonists of these films use their bodies and minds to beat the system and to remain the individuals that they are. The hero status of Brennick and Robbins forms a contrast to other characters, however. Because they do not refuse to be subjectified as prisoners, the heroes' African American counterparts in particular—Abraham and Hawkins—do not embody the characteristics of empowered prisoners.[13]

As mentioned above, Abraham is a passive slave-like subject to cyborgs and technology. He has a role in Brennick's escape plan not as an escaping partner, but as a helping hand to ensure Karen and John Brennick's successful exit from the facility. As the Chief of Security, Hawkins is the second in command after Father, but Robbins usurps his position when Father dies; Hawkins is easily manipulated by Robbins, the newcomer who supposedly ranks low in the Insider community where merit and power can only be earned through long term service to the community. Robbins, however, asserts his power by ignoring Father's deathbed wish for him to become the new leader, and instead tells Hawkins that he is to take Father's place. In effect, then, Robbins gives Hawkins second-hand what seems to be rightfully his—his position as Father—but denies him the ultimate dream of all prisoners, the chance to get away. Therefore, Hawkins' subjectivity as a prisoner depends less on his own agency than on Robbins' actions. When Robbins, with a few other Insiders, escapes the prison island, he takes Father's emblem of power, his diary, the most important document about the unethical manner of mass incarceration on Absolom, and thus Robbins symbolically becomes Father after all. Furthermore, having secured Marek's machine gun and Father's diary, Robbins commands both the phallic and intellectual property of the community and thus proves the superiority of white masculinity.

The black-white opposition in the promotion of new prisoner subjectivities demonstrates the boundaries of the resistance and escape that contemporary futuristic prison films suggest. Since only the white male—who does not belong in prison in the first place because his crime makes him innocent—can escape and assume the position of the hero, the resistance, to some extent, seems like a *fantasy* of resistance. Although futuristic films promote new prisoner identities, they fail to go further to challenge the racialized power structures and hierarchies of masculinity dominant in the majority of American cultural production.[14] In a way, by retaining prison escape as a *fantasy* of white American manhood, the films also retain the Foucaultian framework of there not being any "outside" to the system. For the majority of the male characters, criminality remains embedded in their subjectivity, and therefore they deserve the punishment of being possessed or destroyed by the system of imprisonment.

The emphasis on super-masculine characters suggesting new forms of prisoner subjectivity in futuristic prison films contrasts sharply with the victimization or dehumanization depicted in documentaries that extrapolate the future of imprisonment in the United States. *The Farm: Life Inside Angola Prison* expresses a lot of sympathy toward its inmates by individualizing them and by treating them as men whose lives deserve attention. The film makes an effort to show, for example, how inmates can improve the quality of their lives (the rest of which they are likely to spend in the Angola maximum security prison) by pursuing educational or religious activities, through which they may earn the right to visit and educate people outside the prison, and by so doing "give back to the community."

Even so, *The Farm* ends up victimizing inmates by showing their helplessness when they are faced with the State of Louisiana legislation, for which "life" means "life," and with the parole board that seems to never parole. The narrative makes the viewers feel the disappointment and help-lessness of the prisoners by showing intimate glimpses into their hopes and aspirations. The interviewer is not visible in the film and, when the intervie-wee speaks directly to the camera, he seems to be having a conversation with the audience.

The story of Vincent Simmons is particularly effective in the way it enables the audience to experience the buildup of hope and the consequent disappointment. Simmons is a middle-aged, self-educated man who is working to have his court case re-opened—he was convicted of raping two women, one of whom said in an interview with the police that she would not be able to recognize her assailant because "all of them niggers look alike"—and preparing for his parole board hearing. When he speaks to the camera about the new evidence he has been able to unearth, Simmons seems very confident. The film then shows Simmons addressing the parole board with his hands cuffed, which makes it difficult for him to organize his paperwork. After a very brief hearing, he is escorted out of the room, and the viewers continue to see and hear the members of the board discuss his case. The film has a candid camera-like feel because the viewers—who were previously engaged in an intimate conversation with Simmons—now eavesdrop on a discussion concerning him that he is not allowed to hear. Because the viewers also hear that he is denied parole before he does, they are inclined to pity him rather than to admire his efforts.

The Farm also seems to victimize prisoners by representing them through the metaphor of slavery. In the case of Angola, this metaphor is virtually unavoidable: the prison is located on the property of a former plantation and is named for the place from which the slaves on the planta-tion originated. One scene, in particular, evokes the notion that there is not much difference between pursuing capital gain by enslaving or impris-oning men; the production strategies indirectly connect the institutions of slavery, mass incarceration, and capitalism. While the video depicts the predominantly African American prisoners working on the fields with primitive tools like forks and hoes—with armed "overseers" on horseback policing them—the audio voice-over alternates between Warden Cain and the narrator commenting in a detached documentary-like manner on the conditions in Angola. Because the alternating voices complement each other, the commentary is subtly ironic. The narrator speaks about how Angola used to be a plantation, how the prisoners all work every day in the fields—for four cents a day, starting at 5 A.M.—and how the prison is a "multi-million business." Warden Cain, on the other hand, implicitly con-gratulates himself for being a good businessman for successfully running such a large establishment, and comments on how good manual labor is for the morale of prisoners who may have "illusions of grandeur of driving a tractor one day." To complete the picture of black people going through hard times, the score is comprised of spirituals and blues songs. By combining the elements of work, capital, slavery, and imprisonment, the film critiques prisons as businesses that thrive by working their prisoners in slavery-like conditions.

The manner in which *The Farm* depicts prisoners as victims fits, to some extent, its obvious didactic aims and probably also reflects the somewhat delicate environment of its filming and production. Film crews are seldom allowed in prisons and, when they are, they have to work according to and around the conditions set by the correctional institution—particularly when, as is the case with *The Farm,* one of its inmates, Wilbert Rideau, is the co-director. Other elements demonstrating the film's didactic position are, perhaps, its focus on how escapees from this prison are always quickly caught and how men who end up in Angola are likely to die there.

While *The Farm* portrays prisoners through the metaphor of slavery, "Crime and Punishment" dehumanizes prisoners by representing them as mentally disturbed, animal-like creatures, even though paradoxically, its object appears to be to show that prisoners are human beings who should not be treated in a manner that turns them into animals in the prisons "of the future." Ted Koppel critiques modern maximum-security facilities for isolating prisoners from each other and reducing all human contact to "absolute minimum." At the same time, a major problem that "Crime and Punishment" illustrates is confrontations between the members of the prison population, and between prisoners and correctional officers. To solve this problem, the "supermax" prisons offer more isolation—"administrative segregation"—where men are placed in conditions that are repeatedly described as "not human."

The "human-not human" rhetoric is typical of prison narratives, although traditionally the question of prisoners' humanity is discussed in terms of prisoners being something less than human (or even animal-like) simply because they are in prison. Various sociological and psychological studies have supported the claim that there exists a sub-class of crime prone individuals who are identifiable either by their genetic composition or their upbringing. "Crime and Punishment," together with several fictive representations of imprisonment, on the other hand, seems to argue that prisoners are, indeed, human, when they enter the prison, but that the correctional treatment turns them into less than human madmen who need to be locked up. According to "Crime and Punishment," the isolation in maximum security prisons is said to "frustrate" and "drive men mad—literally," and prison officials are concerned about releasing the "strain of madness," that, according to the narrator, "lies just beneath the surface of the masks [the prisoners] show." Thus, the documentary seems to argue that the prisoners need to be incarcerated not because of the crimes that they committed but because of the treatment they received in correctional facilities.

In Part 3 of the documentary series "Crime and Punishment," "Welcome to the Prison of the Future" (filmed in a supermax prison in Huntsville, Texas), a prisoner interviewed by Ted Koppel compares the facility to "those Nazi concentration camps" and says that he is concerned about his mental health. The prisoner is in the administrative segregation unit for disobeying the rules of the prison by refusing to comply with a body search, a routine procedure in the facility. He rationalized his behavior by saying that not obeying the rules is a strategy for not losing his manhood.

Part 3 and Part 4, "Blood in, blood out—you'll meet the Mexican Mafia," touch upon the racial and cultural differences between prisoners. A prison official explains that more than half of the men are in administrative segregation because they are *believed to be* members of the murderous prison gang . . . the largest and most dangerous prison gang in the country . . . the Mexican Eme" (my italics). The correctional officer also remarks that the members of this murderous gang are the "most well-behaved and polite in the administrative segregation." Taken together, these remarks suggest that these prisoners are isolated primarily because of their ethnic background. One of the prisoners interviewed in the documentary identifies himself as a member of an organization that works from inside the prison. Interestingly, he says that the gang offers him *mental* support, not the physical protection that might be expected to be needed by a member of a gang defined as "murderous." Thus, the documentary focuses on the issue of mental health both from the point of view of prisoners' own concerns about the effects of total isolation and from the point of view of the outcome itself—losing one's mind, and therein, one's humanity.

By depicting inmates as victims and controllable subjects of the U.S. prison system, documentaries like *The Farm* and "Crime and Punishment" contrast sharply with futuristic films that propose new empowered subjectivities for prisoners. In the documentaries, some prisoners are shown to resist by "refusing"—like the inmate who refuses the body search—but they are quickly turned into disciplinary objects that can be classified, manipulated, and controlled through strategies that Foucault describes as techniques of individualizing and totalizing power. *The Farm* seems to point out that individual effort is not enough to beat the system—"the Man"—that controls the judicial system. "Crime and Punishment" shows men locked up in their small cells for 23 hours a day, yelling and screaming like animals, under the permanent gaze of surveillance cameras, and spending their daily "recreational" hour in individual cages. If a prisoner refuses to comply with discipline, he may be locked up in a "sensory deprivation" cell in which he loses his sense of time. All these techniques demonstrate the dehumanizing effects of imprisonment in what Ted Koppel calls "the prisons of the future."

While documentary films explore the essence of humanness by suggesting that the current conditions of U.S. prisons severely dehumanize inmates, futuristic prison films take the perspective typical of science fiction and examine the boundaries of humanity by focusing on relationships between humans and various non-human life forms. These films project the fantasy of crossing the border between human and machine both by representing prisoners as aliens themselves and representing prisoners in contact with non-human life. Ridley Scott's *Blade Runner* (1982) imagines a future with cyborg "replicants" who are enslaved by humans living on Mars, and who—when they escape—are tracked down like escaped prisoners. In Nicholas Meyer's *Star Trek VI: The Undiscovered Country* (1991), Captain Kirk and Dr. McCoy become imprisoned in "gulag Rura Pente" with prisoners representing various alien life forms. In Marco Brambilla's *Demolition Man* (1993), inmates are rehabilitated in a sub-zero "behavioral engineering complex" that alters the prisoners' behavior and in some cases also provides them with superior knowledge and powers when they are "reanimated." In David Fincher's *Alien 3* (1992), the prison is a spaceship, replicating the future of the tradition of expelling and transporting convicts to far away criminal colonies in the future.

Fortress takes a different approach to examining humans in contact with non-humans by placing the humans *not* in control of alien bodies, but as objects for cyborgs' experimentation with human life. Since having more than one child is a criminal act, women pregnant with a second child become the property of MEN-TEL Corporation and their newborn babies objects for "enhancement" that will make humans more durable and almost maintenance-free. The prisoners themselves are used as prosthetic devices for cyborg-guards. These "perfect soldiers"—who, in a sense, are also prisoners guarding themselves—are created by wiring the prisoners' brains into the central-control mainframe and by arming them with machine guns that are directly attached to their bodies. *Fortress* thus represents the fear of machines taking over by exploring the possibility of humans losing the authorship to breach the boundary between human and machine; in the future it will be the machines that do that.

As an apocalyptic narrative of cyborg take-over, *Fortress* is not ready for the postmodernist or posthumanist celebration of "enhanced" human potential, or what Donna Haraway calls a "cyborg world" of "social and bodily realities in which people are not afraid of their joint kinship with animals and machines, not afraid of permanently partial identities and contradictory standpoints" (154).[15] *Fortress* retains the integrity of human identity by contrasting Karen and John Brennick to the techno-couple, Director Poe (who was born and enhanced in the institution and has never left the premises) and his female counterpart, Zed-10. By addressing the issue of procreation—one not commonly raised in prison narratives—the film claims that any "joint kinship" with machines or machine-like beings would be horrifying and unnatural.

This claim points toward two interrelated, but separate issues. First, the narrative of *Fortress* suggests that a state and a criminal justice system that passes and enforces laws criminalizing reproduction and allowing a correctional facility to own and experiment on the unlawfully procreated babies is an inhumane system that deprives innocent people their freedom and humanness. Poe and Zed-10, as mechanized beings unmoved by human feelings and suffering, work as the primary executioners of the laws. Their position as entities exerting the highest power in the institution—with the cyborg guards as their minions—makes the prison system itself seem alien. Second, the film suggests that to preserve humanness the future needs uncontrolled, purely *human* reproduction, and therefore relationships between humans and machines, and the cyborg-like offspring thereof, are unthinkable.[16] The film's anti-genetic engineering stance challenges the masculinist tradition in science fiction that, ever since Mary Shelley's *Frankenstein,* imagines technological reproduction without females.

Although it first seems that Karen and John Brennick are simply victims of cyborg experimentation, the issue of procreation inverts the balance of power. Despite their status as an enhanced male and a seemingly all-powerful female, Poe and Zed-10 are not capable of reproduction without humans—the pleasures of sex and drinking alcohol are not programmed into enhanced beings—and therefore they need couples like Karen and John. This is evident in the scenes where Poe first demands that Karen Brennick become his "companion" in order to save her husband's life, and later proposes to Karen, so that he, Karen, and her baby can live as a family.

In the end, the seeming seduction (only Karen knows that Poe is incapable of sexual intercourse) of a human female by a cyborg male reasserts the masculinity of the hero, John Brennick, and the cyborg world is presented as another obstacle he must overcome on his quest for freedom. Even though Poe uses the on-screen images of Karen for his voyeuristic pleasures, he is impotent, and so John—as Karen's sole sexual partner—retains his masculinity. John's masculinity is further asserted by his action as the instigator of the prison breakout. His experience as an army officer provides him with skills that enable him to plan and execute the escape, although his experience as a *failed* officer makes him reluctant to include others in his plan and be "responsible for another man's life again." He only agrees to his allow cellmates to accompany him because he needs their output for executing the plan.

The manner in which individual output is divided during the escape follows traditional gender roles. Although Karen is an ex-army computer technician and has previously used Zed-10, it is a male character—D-Day (Jeffrey Combs)—and not Karen, who hacks into the computer system to facilitate her escape. D-Day is the computer specialist, John the expert on military skills that include leadership, intelligence, and physical force. Karen, conversely, is the pregnant woman who needs to be saved from the hands of Poe and his staff by her husband. Karen previously saved John's life by acting according to her role as a female—by using her body—and accepting Poe's offer to become his "companion."

The male-female opposition also plays a part in illustrating the vulnerability of the prison surveillance system and the superior intelligence of the male and part-human Poe to the female and mechanical Zed-10. When the breakout is in progress, Zed-10 tells Director Poe that he is being replaced because of his failure to detect the escape plan. At this point, Poe also learns that his "private quarters" have been under continuous surveillance, and that he no longer has access to Zed-10—she is in control until Poe's replacement arrives. While in control, however, Zed-10 unknowingly provides the escape route for Brennick and his cellmates by blowing a hole in the prison ventilation system. The reason for her error is her lack of the human (and male) capability of reasoning and her failure to use her visual surveillance data in a creative manner. Poe, on the contrary, shows his human and male weakness by becoming infatuated with Karen Brennick despite Zed-10's warnings that the relationship would not be beneficial to the Corporation. In this particular dialogue between Zed-10 and Poe, Zed-10's previously conversational tone becomes highly laconic and mechanized, which suggests that her warning is motivated by jealousy. Thus, human-cyborg relationships are presented as detrimental, not only from the human point of view, but also from the point of view of the cyborgs and the prison, since human emotions and weaknesses inhibit their functioning as well.

The system breakdown also demonstrates that, despite its sophisticated surveillance and communication technologies, the prison as a system is only seemingly in control of its own operation. The various workings of power and control are reminiscent of Foucaultian mazes of power and knowledge in which a single source for ultimate power does not exist. Poe, as the director of the institution, has a certain amount of power, but the invisible global ownership of MEN-TEL—personified as the voice and eye of Zed-10—oversees his actions. As such, Poe is confined by the Corporation and his behavior is monitored and controlled in much the same way as is the prisoners' behavior. Zed-10's error, however, is as damaging to the system as a human error and therefore shows that technology cannot provide infallible solutions for control either. The prisoners, in contrast, are able to turn the prison's central control unit to work for rather than against them, although all the men involved in the breakout—with the exception of John Brennick—lose their lives. In the final scenes of the film, the last attempt of the prison to regain control comes from an unexpected source: the truck that was used to transport the prisoners activates itself into a killing machine, with the remaining prisoners—Karen, John, and Nino—as its targets. John manages to destroy the machine that has killed Nino while Karen is giving birth to their baby. With the nuclear family restored, the Brennicks escape to begin a new life in primitive Mexico.

By projecting the future prison back into the primitive, science fiction films refers nostalgically to the past in various ways. First, both *No Escape* and *Fortress* equate the return to a past with a pastoral coexistence of man and nature. The last moments of *Fortress* show John and Karen Brennick in a nativity scene-like harmony with their newborn baby in rural Mexico. Also, John's deteriorated appearance suggests a primitive existence: his unkempt "Tarzan" hair and his torn clothes are evocative of the times of the cavemen. Also, *No Escape*, with its starting-from-scratch spirit, takes us back to the times of *Robinson Crusoe* and man's struggle for survival in a wilderness that challenges, but also provides.

Second, the films often represent a primitive, survival-of-the-fittest concept of justice. The prisoners are dropped on remote islands where they either receive small "rations" from the government or must find other ways of surviving, and often must defend themselves against attacks by other prisoners. Herley's *The Penal Colony* explains the resort to primitive law by the fact that island colonies are cheaper than maximum-security prisons—the government "economizes" on its "dirty work" by letting the inmates kill each other off (150, 299). Thus, the films reflect a popular solution to the problems of war and crime—the idea of isolating warmongers and killers and from the general population and letting them eliminate each other for the benefit of the rest of society.

Third, the films refer to a return to the primitive national past of the United States, to the narrative of new frontiers and the settling of the West. As Andrew Ross points out in "Cowboys, Cadillacs and Cosmonauts: Families, Film Genres, and Technocultures," "science-fiction films today increasingly borrow more conventions from the Western than from the horror genres that were their primary source in the 1950s" (95). By doing so, these films speak to the "foundational myths of masculine and national identity" while retaining their "racist mythologies" (95). This is, indeed, how futuristic prison films operate. The films criticize the current trends of imprisonment through celebrating the nationalistic ideals of freedom and American white male individualism and heroism. The maverick prisoner-heroes solve the problem of unjust imprisonment by escaping from it to new frontiers. The nationalistic ideal of freedom is apparent in the Brennicks' finding freedom and a new beginning in Mexico, while in *No Escape* the scope is larger: the new frontier Robbins sets out for is an international community that will help him to create a new, less corrupt beginning for the U.S. criminal justice system.

Another way that science fiction prison films promote new kinds of prisoner identity is in their treatment of homosexuality. The tension in the representation of homosexuality in the films seems to indicate that a cultural reconfiguration of male relationships in a homosocial space is conceivable. While most prison films still represent homosexuality as a perversion that affirms criminality—or infinite guilt—some recent films, to some degree, display a homoerotic tension that offers a less homophobic view of sexuality in all-male environments. These films challenge the opposition between the heterosexual and homosexual and reshape the concept of the male hero by representing him as sexually superior—both as a normative male and as an object for homoerotic desire. This double-take on homosexuality in prison films illustrates Linda Singer's theory, presented in *Erotic Welfare,* of how the outside (homosexuality) is both excluded from the inside (heterosexuality) and produced by it (3–7). In prison films, the homophobic ideology both excludes male-male sex as perversion, and simultaneously fetishizes it as an object of fascination within the realm of male sexuality.

Fortress, on the one hand, exemplifies the typical treatment of homosexuality in prison films: male-male sex both as excluded and fetishized through the homophobic representation of male-male rape and conflicts caused by homosexual innuendo. The very first incidents suggesting or displaying violence in the film involve a reference to male-male sexual acts. As a newcomer to the prison, Brennick proves his manhood by first repelling his cellmate Stiggs' sexual advances and later by interrupting the rape of Nino by Maddox, Stiggs' partner. The final revenge and abolition of homosexuality, however, comes from the prison system. While Brennick is satisfied with having solved the conflict by fighting off the rapist, and by doing so, asserting his heterosexuality, Poe does not think having been beaten up is punishment enough for Maddox and orders Zed-10 to kill the rapist. Thus homosexuality, and by implication the possibility of male-male rape, is obliterated by eliminating the man personifying it. This narrative treatment both includes the thrill of rape and demonstrates that the surviving, heroic masculinity is heterosexual.

No Escape, on the other hand, illustrates a hierarchy of sexual difference that is atypical of prison films. Although the film retains some of the phobic vision in its characterization of the Outsiders—and their leader Marek in particular—as rapists, it also foregrounds a relationship involving deep male-male feelings and visual homoerotic tension. Casey (Kevin Dillon)—marked as a "boy" by being identified by only a first name in a community where all other members call each other "Mr."—plays a part in every major moment of Robbins' life on the prison island, and their relationship—the only one that carries through the whole narrative—evolves from one-sided hero worship into intimate mutual friendship.[17]

Casey and Robbins' intimacy develops in a sequence of three scenes that resonate with sexually charged passion and devotion. The first takes place after Robbins has saved Casey's life in combat with the Outsiders. In addition to being a boy, Casey is also different from other male characters in that he is shown to be fearful in battle. In a scene back-lit with bursts of fire meant to destroy the Insider community, Casey and Robbins stand face to face—Robbins touches Casey gently, and comforts him in a soft voice. The moment is private and quiet after the tumultuous, noisy battle scene.

The next scene showing the growing intimacy between the two men takes place in the woods where Casey has followed Robbins because he wants to accompany him on his trip to the Outsider camp. In a backlit close-up, Robbins grabs Casey, pushes him against a tree, and in a passionate voice tries to convince Casey not to follow him. Again, the scene is quiet; the shot-reverse-shot technique alternates between close-ups of both men's faces, full of excitement, with glistening eyes, and panting for suppressed emotions. The scene is typical in romantic films, with the exception that this couple does not kiss and embrace, the expected next step in a film about a male-female couple.

In the third scene, the embrace that finally takes place also kills Casey. In spite of Robbins' pleas, Casey follows him, and as a result both get caught by Marek's men. Marek further affirms Casey's position as an object of male desire by gazing up and down at his body and simultaneously calling him a "sweet, tender, adorable little boy." Marek makes Casey and Robbins fight each other in a gladiator-like manner in a deep pool of water—the winner of the battle will have the chance to save his life. After Casey urges Robbins to kill him (so that he can go back and "save" the Insider community), Robbins thrusts a knife through his body. In a close-up embrace, with their bodies and hair glistening wet from water, both men are again panting heavily, with Casey voicing, "no, no." The scene combines elements characteristic of the representation of the sexual act—the embrace, the penetration, the panting, and the passionate utterances, together with association of death with orgasm.

Although it might seem that Robbins "kills" his male-male desire by killing Casey, his feelings towards him are alluded to in the final scene of the film in which he flies off the island in a helicopter. In his last, sad glimpse of the island Robbins focuses on Casey's favorite spot on it—the spot he calls "wet dreams." The ending thus combines the two main topics of the movie: escape and a male friendship that has erotic undertones.

Even so, *No Escape* dilutes its seeming acceptance of homosexuality by introducing another category in the hierarchy of male sexual difference. The character of Tom King (Ian McNeice) is portrayed as the stereotypic gay man. He is represented as domestic and weak and, therefore feminized: he speaks in a lisping manner (with a British accent) and tells Robbins to wipe his feet when he enters his house while he is dusting it; he is also fearful in battle and a hypochondriac. In the end, homosexuality becomes criminalized when it is revealed that King is not only the Warden's lover but also his spy on the island. The criminal gay couple gets its punishment at the end of the film when the two men are left standing alone as targets for the savage Outsiders. Since Robbins is the only man who ever escaped from Marek and his men, it is certain that these men will be eliminated. Although *No Escape,* like *Fortress,* excludes homosexuality by erasing it through killing its gay characters, it simultaneously promotes male-male relationships that are not openly sexual, but display homoerotic desire. By representing a broadened concept of male sexual difference in this manner, the film suggests a less homophobic reading of prison sexuality.

Jameson's claim that, by projecting the problems of today into the future, science fiction makes it easier to deal with the present applies to the films discussed above. The spatial and temporal narrative distancing in these films defamiliarizes the perception of the present by restructuring a cultural experience of incarceration as a cornerstone of the U.S. criminal justice system. The apocalyptic visions of the future corrections systems that these films project are, in fact, conservative compared to the *present* reported by documentaries such as *The Farm* and "Crime and Punishment." Recent television news about prison riots and accusations of continuing violations of prisoners' civil rights also testify to the unbearable conditions of contemporary maximum security prisons.[18] The factual present of prisons in the United States is thus already worse than their imagined future.

From another point of view, the documentaries themselves can be seen to project the present into the future. *The Farm* emphasizes the need for geriatric wards in prisons as a problem of the future, even though the aging of the prison population is already visible in the film. Ted Koppel titles one of the parts of "Crime and Punishment" "Welcome to the Prison of the Future," but he is clearly interviewing inmates and staff in an already existing facility. The future that these documentaries depict is actually the present. Although the aim of these films seems to be to inform the public of present conditions in U.S. prisons, their narrative techniques of spatial and temporal distancing alleviate the fear of crime and criminals by relocating them into the distant future. As long as the viewers are invited to perceive prisons as isolated islands outside of society and to feel comfortable knowing that those crazy men are *not yet* roaming the streets of their neighborhoods, they can think that they still have time to do something about the problem—or they can simply forget about it and let the future take care of it.

Criminologists, however, sound a stronger warning. Michael Tonry, in his introduction to *The Handbook of Crime and Punishment* (1998), does not specify his prediction for the future of American corrections, but he does caution that, until "fundamental policy changes are made, the seemingly inexorable increases in incarceration and the grossly disproportionate presence of blacks in prisons and jails will continue" ("Crime" 24). He also implies that "American crime policies" were more "effective and more humane" in the America of "other times" and are so in other Western countries today (24). Tonry outlines his critique by pointing out practices that have caused American penal policy to reach its less effective and less humane state, and that may cause it to remain that way in the future.

Tonry blames political decision makers for having been "conspicuously uninterested in evaluation research showing that politically popular programs are ineffective" ("Crime" 7). As one example of ineffective legislation, he cites mandatory minimum prison sentences for drug dealers, which do not "reduce drug abuse or availability" (7, citing Wilson). The reason politicians lack interest in research on crime polices, Tonry claims, is "ideological conviction, partisan politics, political symbolism [fear of being labeled as 'soft' on crime], or distrust of researchers" (7). He also claims that, due to practical considerations, few "judges and informed scholars" support laws such as the "three-strikes-and-you're-out laws" and "sexual psychopath" laws—these laws are too "rigid," and therefore result in "unjustly harsh penalties" (5–6).

According to Tonry, the *representation* of crime in politics and in the media may have "precipitated," and not just reflected, "the public concern about crime and public support for harsh policies" ("Crime" 5). Since the media continues to focus on the most horrifying criminal cases, representing them sensationalistically and realistically, and politicians continue to emphasize the problem of crime, public awareness of crime is heightened and average citizens perceives crime rates to be growing year by year (13, citing Maguire and Pastore, table 2.27). Tonry acknowledges that the "apologists'" views favoring harsh policies have some validity as well—the public "anxiety about crime is real," crime issues are important, and thus the "public benefits both from being alerted to them and from the adoption of new policies aimed at reducing crime" (5).

By transgressing the current popular images of prisoners as inhuman garbage, futuristic prison films promote new forms of prisoner subjectivity. This promotion is evident in the manner in which these films depict characters who successfully refuse to comply with the techniques of individualizing and totalizing power that the state—or correctional institutions as its representatives—use to objectify and control prisoners as subjects. The new prison subjectivities that these films promote are exclusive in terms of race and gender, however. The male who defeats the flawed criminal justice system is always white, and the few non-white characters exist only through their relationship with the white male hero, not as characters in their own right.

Although futuristic prison films differ from traditional prison films in that they include female characters, the conventional gender roles affirm the masculinist desire for control typical of science fiction. The characterization of females, like that of non-white characters, primarily reasserts the masculinity of the male characters. *No Escape* is a traditional prison film in the sense that the narrative obliterates femininity, while *Fortress* uses its female characters to boost the heroic qualities of the male protagonists and to confirm the status of the nuclear family as a social and cultural icon.

Stephanie Rothman's *Terminal Island* (1973)—the precursor of futuristic prison films portraying prisons as primitive island communities—is radical in its focus on coed prison life, and yet it characterizes female protagonists as sex-slaves for male prisoners; or, as the character of Joy Lang (Phyllis Davis) puts it, "We're the property of every man on the island." This tendency to see women in prison only in a sexual context also has contributed to making women-in-prison films (with titles such as *Caged Heat, Bad Girls Dormitory,* and *The Big Doll House*) a genre of its own. While these women-in-prison films typically depict female characters as victims of sexual assault, the films discussed above use female characters as vehicles through which the male characters' heroic masculinity is reinforced.

The kind of re-evaluation and broadening of concepts and value systems achieved in terms of crime and criminality has not yet taken place in terms of race and gender in science fiction prison film. These films promote and celebrate a limited new form of prisoner subjectivity—that of the outlaw male individual who aspires to a new, just beginning—but, because they fail to recognize the complexities of race and gender within that subjectivity, they continue the tradition of racist and sexist representation. However, as the example of Casey and Robbins' homoerotic relationship shows, futuristic prison films seem to open the door to reconfigurations of male-male prison sexuality and the new ways of looking at sexual difference that they offer.

Chapter Two

African American Prison Autobiography: From Racial to Sexual Politics

The recent interest in reinvestigating the guilt and innocence of prisoners has caused a revival in the genre of prison autobiographical writing. Advancements in forensic methods such as DNA testing have led to the reopening of an increasing number of criminal cases, which in turn has generated new autobiographical narratives and the republication of earlier ones. The reopening of the murder case of Rubin "Hurricane" Carter, the internationally known African American boxer, for example, generated new interest in his autobiographical narratives. Carter was released from prison after having been wrongfully incarcerated for nineteen years (*The Hurricane Carter Story*). Besides his personal testimonies of imprisonment, his release created several other products, among them Norman Jewison's film, *The Hurricane* (1999), which is based, in part, on Carter's 1974 autobiography, *The Sixteenth Round: From Number 1 Contender to # 45472*. The film recognizes the act of autobiographical writing in prison as a "weapon more powerful than a fist," and claims that the manuscript for Carter's autobiography would be his "only way out" of prison. The autobiography in fact turned out to be the instrument for Carter's way out. His case was reopened due to the efforts of a group of Canadian liberals who heard about Carter from Lesra Martin, a young black boy from Brooklyn who had read Carter's book and resolved to make a difference.

Recent scholarly and popular interest in the political activism of the 1960s and 1970s and in the Black Power Movement in particular has resulted in the republication of writings such as George Jackson's *Soledad Brother: The Prison Letters of George Jackson*, originally published in

1970 and reprinted in 1994. A notable recent contribution to the study of the autobiographical writing from that period is Margo V. Perkins' *Autobiography as Activism: Three Black Women of the Sixties* (2000). Perkins' primary focus is on the work of Angela Davis, Assata Shakur, and Elaine Brown, but she also considers their autobiographical writing in the context of autobiographies of their male contemporaries such as Malcolm X and Eldridge Cleaver.

Prison autobiographies satisfy the public curiosity about the intricacies of the U.S. criminal justice system, but they also work as a discursive site for satisfying voyeuristic pleasures. Although seemingly peripheral, life in prison has become an issue central to the American experience, and therefore also is central as a cultural fantasy. Firsthand narratives of life behind the bars provide mainstream audiences the opportunity to go "slumming" in prison in much the same way that the Victorian upper class went into the poverty-ridden areas of London, as described by Peter Stallybrass and Allon White in *The Politics and Poetics of Transgression* (1986). Thus, prison autobiography proposes to its reader a self-congratulatory social narrative that reinforces the categories of the social "high"—the world outside the prison—and "low"—the world inside.

Within the context of offering a transgressive reinforcement for the security and values of middle class life, prison autobiography, as a social symbolic, also re-convinces the public of the necessity of prisons as rehabilitative institutions. The most popular prison autobiographies provide success stories of people whose lives altered during their prison terms. The most celebrated and most imitated of these inspirational prison autobiographies is *The Autobiography of Malcolm X* (1964). Texts by ex-inmates who became professional writers during their time in prison—authors such as Chester Himes and Nathan C. Heard, for instance—also testify to the reformative qualities of imprisonment.

While prison autobiographies invite social voyeurism—by privileging the ones outside of the narrative as the norm, or the social "high"—they also serve as outlets for the fantasy of homosexual encounters in prison. Thus the "gaze" from the outside of the narrative affirms social and moral hierarchies by identifying the subject of the narrative as both morally and sexually perverse.

Since one element of the public cultural fascination about life in prison appears to be same-sex rape, contemporary prison autobiographies necessarily focus on this issue. Prison narratives tend to polarize male-male rape by representing the rapist as a brutal sexual predator and the victim as an effeminate "punk" who has lost his manhood. Now that prison rape has become an acceptable topic, even on early-evening television news programs such as ABC's "Tonight with Peter Jennings," prison autobiographers are facing the problem of how to narrate their experiences of masculinity and sexuality in prison—how to situate themselves as the subject in control of the narrative rather than as an object of simultaneous fascination and repugnance. How the autobiographer situates himself in the imaginary of prison rape and simultaneously retains his sense of masculinity is a focal point of this chapter.

My analysis of African American prison autobiographies involves four major arguments. First, in terms of male-on-male rape I challenge the notion that rape is primarily an act of establishing power hierarchies, not a question of sexuality, as argued in heterosexual contexts and also in most non-autobiographical prison narratives.[1] I demonstrate how rape in prison autobiography is not mainly a question of masculine power and control by focusing on the subjectivity of the rapist, which is simultaneously hypermasculine and stigmatized in prison autobiography.

Second, I argue that the problem of male sexuality and the maintenance of the structure of male dominance in an all male environment is indicative of a discursive and social crisis of male representation in contemporary prison autobiography. At a time when an increasing number of African American men spend most of their active adult lives in prison, and when the issue of prison sexuality is publicly discussed, prison autobiographical writing serves as a defense of black manhood in which the authors negotiate between the reality of their lives and the cultural fascination and phobia with homosocial spaces.

My third argument is that the provisionality, or instability, of prison masculinity—and of prison sexuality in particular—that prison autobiographies display promotes what Kaja Silverman calls the "dominant fiction": the patriarchal ideology of stability of heterosexuality and family (15–51). While prison autobiographies narrate homosexual eroticism and encounters in prison, they simultaneously aim at convincing readers that their in-prison sexual orientation is only temporary. Therefore, they formulate prison masculinity as a provisional state and, by so doing, advocate the stability of heterosexuality.

Finally, I argue that, even though prison autobiographies suggest a subversive, non-homophobic version of masculinity by focusing on homosexual relations as a norm, their accounts are mostly non-subversive because of the narrative strategies they use. The authors, for example, tend to deny their own involvement in any subversive acts—to deny that they are among the "almost all" prisoners who get raped in prison, for instance. Situating homosexuality outside the realm of one's own subjectivity again objectifies it as something non-normative and, as such, as a source for phobia.

Even autobiographical narratives in publications such as the web-based *Stop Prisoner Rape* that do represent rape victims may have unintended representational consequences. Stop Prisoner Rape, Inc. is a national non-profit organization that supports a website focusing on the problem of rape in prison, with the aim of educating prisoners, the general public, and incarceration professionals (1). *Stop Prisoner Rape* argues that "rape is a crime of power which cannot alter the victim's masculinity or sexual orientation" (2). Yet one of the prisoner-authors, a self-declared heterosexual, writes that, "I have to confess that getting fucked by a tender, gentle jock was better than the vicious gang-bangs and *there was pride in making my man happy in bed*" ("The Story of a Black Punk," my italics). Thus, even a publication geared toward speaking for rape survivors and making male-male rape an acceptable topic of discussion may both generate homophobia and reinforce the notion that prisoners are uncertain about their masculinity.

It is no surprise that a significant number of contemporary autobiographical prison narratives are written by African American authors. According to recent statistics 2,149,900 adults, or nine percent of the African American population is currently under correctional supervision,[2] and over fifty percent of U.S. inmates are black. It is not surprising either that prison autobiography is a prominent subgenre of African American writing: African Americans have a long history of being detained and incarcerated, and this has generated narratives that form a distinct category. Any list of seminal African American autobiographical writings includes prison narratives—from classic texts such as Frederick Douglass' *Narrative of the Life of Frederick Douglass, An American Slave*, Dr. Martin Luther King, Jr.'s "Letter from a Birmingham Jail,"[3] and *The Autobiography of Malcolm X* to the most recent autobiographical texts by Nathan McCall and Mumia Abu-Jamal. Autobiographical texts by contemporary male African American authors are the primary focus of this chapter.

African American autobiographical writing characteristically focuses on the issue of race and race relations in the United States, both from the point of view of the autobiographical self and from the point of view of the black community. In this sense, African American autobiography differs from what Philippe Lejeune proposes in his already classic work on the genre of autobiography. According to Lejeune, an autobiography is "the retrospective prose narrative that someone writes concerning his own existence, where the focus is on individual life, in particular the story of his personality" (Eakin, "Foreword" viii, citing Lejeune, *L'Autobiographie*, 14). Concerning the factual and fictional modes of discourse, Lejeune also characterizes autobiographical writing as a "pact" between the author and the reader in which "the autobiographer explicitly commits himself or herself not to some impossible historical exactitude but rather to the sincere effort to come to terms and to understand his or her own life" (Eakin, "Foreword" ix, citing Lejeune). Lejeune's idea of a pact between autobiographers and their audiences applies to African American autobiographers as well, but since they tend to link their life stories with a larger social commentary, and therein with a historical project analyzing American racism, their autobiographies are not purely works that aim at understanding individual existence and personality. Tending to see criminality as a national, social, or community issue, African American prison autobiography also counteracts legal discourses that attempt to define criminality as an issue that solely concerns individuals.

The significant body of black prison narratives produced by the Civil Rights era—empowered by the Black Power and the Black Muslim Movements—displays the racial-political struggle of the time by highlighting black-white opposition in American society. The primacy of the political struggle is evident in contemporary critical reviews of these texts. For example, in her critique of Jackson's *Soledad Brother*, Angela Davis describes it as an "analysis of the American Penal system" that has been "an integral part" of African American life (4, 3). Stephen Butterfield, in his acclaimed *Black Autobiography in America* (1974), also celebrates as the "strongest books" those African American autobiographies that "most successfully assimilate and unify personal narrative and political message" (274). The autobiographies that he discusses in this context include Eldridge Cleaver's *Soul on Ice* and George Jackson's *Soledad Brother*.[4]

Significantly, the authors of these books, like other imprisoned members of the Black Panther Party who have published autobiographies, do not see their political agency as diminished by the fact that they are writing in prison,[5] but, on the contrary, consider their texts as even more consequential instruments of change because they testify to the unjust treatment of black Americans. While the autobiographies of more recent prison writers such as Nathan McCall and Sanyika Shakur include this racial and communal element, their concerns reflect the sentiment that the institution of prison has become part of the black community in an overpowering manner. These texts are often concerned with prison sentences as rites of passage for young men in the black community, for example.

The more personal focus of prison autobiographies by African American male writers is black manhood and the ways in which one's masculinity can be retained in a space where, because of the nature of imprisonment itself, expressions of male agency are largely obliterated. There are, however, generational differences between the ways prison autobiographers approach the issue of incarcerated masculinity. Again, combining the personal with the political, the prison autobiographers of the 1960s and 1970s focus on prison masculinity as a transformation process that has both individual and communal implications. In this process of transformation, the imprisoned individual gains both self respect and respect from the community through socially motivated practices such as educating oneself, becoming more involved in religious or spiritual thought, and raising one's political awareness. Cleaver, for example, says that he began to write in prison since he had lost his self-respect and needed to recapture his "pride as a man" (27).

Manhood is also discussed in the context of larger issues that resonate with the political struggles of both the ante-bellum and the Civil Rights eras. In narratives such as Cleaver's, rhetoric that juxtaposes imprisonment and slavery, on the one hand, and black manhood and humanity, on the other, is prevalent. By centering on the affirmations of humanity and manhood of African American men, these texts, produced in the aftermath of the Civil Rights movement, continue the tradition of slave narratives.

In their critique of raced male subjectivity, contemporary African American prison autobiographies address the problem of prison sexuality—an issue that disrupts the notions of both normative masculinity and of homosexuality. While the autobiographies of the 1960s and 1970s may lament the absence of sexual relations in prison, more recent narratives focus on the problematics of the types of sexual relations available: specifically, masturbation and male-male sex, the latter of which is prohibited by correctional institutions.[6] The topic of sexuality is not completely ignored by the earlier generations of prison writers either, but their writing is less individualizing and introspective in nature. In his 1992 preface to Eldridge Cleaver's *Soul on Ice*, Ishmael Reed claims that Cleaver and his cohorts are "paranoid about their manhood" (xvii). *Soul on Ice* indeed approaches the issue of male sexuality in rather a paranoid manner. Cleaver makes homophobic attacks on homosexuality as "sickness" and gynophobic comments about women, particularly about "The Ogre—the white woman," who is the object of the black male fascination and therefore the cause of his demise (100, 20). Cleaver also celebrates his aggressive masculinity by narrating his experiences as a rapist (26).

The takes on prison masculinity outlined above—both that of political activism and of individual sexuality—are noteworthy for their provisionality. In prison, you can "become a man"; a prison sentence may, indeed, be considered a rite of passage. Fittingly, Eldridge Cleaver begins *Soul on Ice* with a chapter entitled, "On Becoming." Malcolm X's autobiography is also a popular model for transformational prison narratives. However, rather than discussing the process of becoming a man in prison, more recent African American prison autobiographies focus on the fear of "losing" one's manhood through male-male rape or of becoming "turned" gay by veteran inmates. Because of these fears, inmates must repeatedly prove their masculinity in order to regain their "suspended" status as men. The means by which one proves one's masculinity vary from assault and rape to modes of specular promotion of manhood. Bodybuilding, sports, and body tattoos, for example, are standard ways to demonstrate one's manly qualities. In fact, in his recent book, *Monster: The Autobiography of an L.A. Gang Member,* Sanyika Shakur structures the narrative of his personal transformation in prison through narcissistic self-evaluation of his body.

To discuss the issue of male sexuality in prison I consider Linda Singer's theory in *Erotic Welfare: Sexual Theory and Politics in the Age of Epidemic* (1992). Singer's method of feminist inquiry—in part a critique of Foucault's non-hierarchical sense of power structures—is based on her claim that the systems of "masculinist regimes" of power simultaneously exclude women and "recirculate" them *within* those systems as "fetishized objects, phantasmatic sites of erotic investment" (Butler 4).[7] I apply Singer's theory to analyze how, in prison narratives, the homophobic "masculinist regimes" of heterosexuality simultaneously exclude homosexuality by recirculating it as a perversion, and fetishizing it as an object of fascination within the realm of prison masculinity.

The way that the regulatory practice of prohibiting same-sex relationships in prisons also seems to spawn counter-regulatory practices is what Singer terms "panic logic" (Butler 6). Drawing on the Foucaultian notion that resistance is a part of power, Singer analyzes the themes of regulation and control, and the regulatory practices that produce what they seek to control (9). She argues that various phantasmatic "epidemic conditions" that are used to rationalize the regulatory impulse have become the very paradigm of power in society (6). Her primary example is AIDS—an epidemic that created the fear of the "outbreak" of various other "epidemics" such as teenage pregnancy and drug abuse that had nothing to do with AIDS, but that within "cultural discourse [were figured] as threatening social phenomena with the capacity to spread" (6). In prison narratives, the disciplining of homosexuality displaces the forbidden male-male interaction with rape. Thus, the logic that supposedly controls homosexual relationships in prison produces and multiplies them for further consumption.

Tomás Almaguer's "Chicano Men: A Cartography of Homosexual Identity and Behavior" (1993) offers a different way of analyzing the specific structure of prison sexuality. Almaguer, discussing the configuration of homosexuality specific to machismo, argues that male-male sexual relations in Chicano culture are "organized through the scripted sexual role that one plays" (257). The male assuming the "active" role in the sexual act is not "stigmatized" as homosexual while the "passive" party is (257). Homosexual relations are thus understood to be acts of power rather than purely sexual acts. Prison autobiographies often represent one of the parties in sexual acts as feminized and submissive, as the weak "punk" or "old lady" of the dominant male. Race also plays a significant role in these representations, since the black male is typically seen as the aggressor in prison rapes as well as the dominant one in stable male-male relationships.[8]

My main primary sources for discussing male sexuality in recent African American prison autobiographies are Nathan McCall's *Makes Me Wanna Holler: A Young Black Man in America* (1994) and Sanyika Shakur's *Monster: The Autobiography of an L.A. Gang Member* (1993). Both works focus on masculinity and male sexuality in the context of prison, but approach it differently. McCall's *Makes Me Wanna Holler*, on the one hand, approaches black masculinity primarily from the point of view of the mind: he comments on the psychological effect that the life in a homosocial community has on his self-esteem and his sense of his sexual identity. Shakur's *Monster*, on the other hand, focuses on the body, although his neo-nationalist ideology of the essence of black manhood is also on display. Before analyzing individual works, I examine features typical of prison autobiographical writing, address the questions of production and agency that are characteristically problematic to prison writing, and discuss how the genre of prison autobiography differs from mainstream autobiography.

The development of Internet publication has significantly increased the amount of prison autobiographical writing that is easily accessible to the general public. Even so, the authors producing these texts still face the problem of either having no access or very limited access to any medium for publishing their narratives.[9] Even when inmate writers use traditional routes of publishing, they have to be inventive about how to get their manuscripts to prospective publishers. Edward Bunker, for example, in *Education of a*

Felon: A Memoir (2000), relates how in his attempt to prevent prison censors from confiscating his manuscript, "a friend of [his] had his boss, the dentist, carry it out" (127). John Edgar Wideman resorted to taping his in-prison interviews with his brother, Robby, and then turning the interviews into a mediated autobiography, *Brothers and Keepers* (1984).

Therefore, one way of characterizing prison autobiography is to focus on its need to be constantly on the lookout for new channels of publication as legislation closes up existing ones by, for example, enforcing laws that deny the inmates the right to collect money from their writings (Franklin 14). Recently, U.S. popular culture has served as a necessary and productive outlet for prison autobiographical narratives. In addition to the Internet, where such politically active inmates as Mumia Abu-Jamal and Sanyika Shakur publish their writings, prison autobiographies are presented to the public in magazines, newsletters, radio shows, television news, rap lyrics, and advertisements. The Italian clothes manufacturer, Benetton, for instance, caused a great deal of controversy—leading to several court cases—by representing photographs and interviews of U.S. death-row inmates in their 2000 advertising campaign.[10]

The manner in which the authors of contemporary prison autobiographical narratives approach the problem of making their narratives available to the public outside the prison walls is comparable to what Michel de Certeau calls "poaching," a practice of "vigilantly [making] use of the cracks" in social and cultural institutions, with the intent of provoking gradual changes in society (37). In *The Practice of Everyday Life* (1984), de Certeau distinguishes between two kinds of practices that have the capacity of inducing change in society—"strategies" and "tactics." "Strategies" are practices that represent institutionalized power, have established forms, are situated in place, and often work as defense mechanisms for retaining their established forms and functions (xix, 34–36). "Tactics"—practices that "poach in" the institutionalized forms of power—represent the "procedures of everyday creativity" (xiv, 37). They make use of time and opportunity, have no access to power, and no established locus, and thus their agency comes from a kind of guerilla war that maneuvers "within the enemy's field of vision" and "within enemy territory" (xiv–xx, 37–39).

Not only the *manner* in which prison autobiographical writers seize any opportunity of getting published—by smuggling out manuscripts or by being interviewed by commercial entrepreneurs, for instance—but also the *function* of the narratives themselves as a discourse working against the institutionalized logic of imprisonment and criminality make them the kinds of practices that de Certeau calls "tactics." In my analogy, then, the agency of prison autobiographical writing would be located in its capacity to operate as "tactics" of resistance, while the various legal, official, and political modes of institutionalized discourses would represent the "strategies" that hold on to processes that normalize imprisonment and criminality, particularly the imprisonment and criminality of African American males.

One factor that may limit the agency of prison autobiographies as a form of tactical resistance is that often writing coming out of prison is not considered "good" literature, if literature at all. The typically evaluative attitude concerning prison narratives is obvious in William Styron's introduction to Bunker's *Education of a Felon*: "Edward Bunker is one of a *small handful* of American writers who have created *authentic literature* out of their experiences as criminals and prisoners" (ix, my italics). Styron does not mention who the rest of the small handful of authors must be, but goes on to say that the "genuine literary achievement" of [Bunker's four] novels is "astonishing" and places him in the "tiny band of American prisoner-writers whose work possesses integrity, craftsmanship, and moral passion in sufficient measure to claim our serious attention" (ix). He also points out that "[u]nlike the majority of American criminals, [Bunker] was born white" (ix). Whether Bunker's race does or does not have any bearing on his "astonishing" achievement as a writer, Styron's message is clear: "authentic" literature with genuine literary merit is not created by the minds of "criminals and prisoners." In the cultural fantasy that different discourses (prison narratives among them) purport, prisoners are poor, uneducated, inarticulate, and illiterate. Thus, evaluative statements like Styron's stem from a conflict between social and cultural value systems—what represents the social "low" cannot represent the cultural "high." The cultural expectations for products of popular culture are different, however, which also, in part, explains the growing number of prison narratives being published through the popular media.

The different expectations for the cultural high and low also seem to affect the status and agency of the autobiographical self in prison writing. Most book-length prison autobiographies—which as books follow the traditional form of the cultural "high"—perhaps by necessity represent the genre of the *Bildungsroman*. It seems necessary for the writers to "earn" their worth as authors through a process of self-betterment before their narratives can be regarded as good literature. Examples of this transformational approach are *The Autobiography of Malcolm X* (1964), in which Malcolm X narrates his life from the position of a prominent political figure, Jarvis Jay Masters' *Finding Freedom* (1997), in which Masters testifies of his spiritual growth, and Nathan McCall's *Makes Me Wanna Holler* (1994), in which McCall traces his growth from a criminal into a respected journalist at the *Washington Post*. Also an "authentification" by a renowned figure, as in the case of Edward Bunker's autobiography, works as a similar proof of the author's worth as a writer of a culturally high, acceptable prison narrative. This feature of authentification, incidentally, again links prison autobiography to slave narratives, since black narratives were often authenticated by white editors. As *Bildungsromans,* or as authenticated narratives, prison autobiographies promote the ideology of rehabilitation and come close to functioning as institutionalized discourses of imprisonment that advocate individual and social reform.

Returning to de Certeau's theory, if prison narratives are a continuum of "practices," the *Bildungsroman* type of prison autobiography would be closer to the "strategic" end of the continuum because to be published it must be validated through documentation of the author's growth from a criminal into an individual worthy of our attention. This kind of manipulation of the literary form, and therein manipulation of the autobiographical self, also diminishes the writer's agency as the author of his text. The popular culture variety of prison autobiography, in contrast, is more clearly "tactical" because it claims its position without defending itself—through a defense of the autobiographical self—due to its presumed status as marginal literature. This division is not, of course, absolute, but it provides another perspective through which the genre of prison autobiographical writing can be defined.

Prison autobiographies are nevertheless marginal in the sense that their authors are members of a minority group as prisoners, and also because they are often, as African Americans or Latinos, members of racial minority groups.[11] Therefore their narratives are doubly marginal as representations of the social "low" and as texts by "minority" writers. Since the experience of being incarcerated is also marginal in that it is unknown to most readers, autobiographers tend to teach us how to read this experience by educating us about prison discourse and culture. Prison autobiographers frequently explain the language of prison life—in *Seven Long Times* Piri Thomas even includes a glossary of prison slang and explains how to interpret patterns of prison behavior.

Prison autobiographies also breach the conventions of the traditional autobiography in the sense that they are often incomplete stories, and as such convey an incomplete, temporary sense of the autobiographical self.[12] What I consider as prison autobiographies in this study do not necessarily cover the whole lives of the authors, but offer fragmented glimpses into the authors' time in prison. Eldridge Cleaver's *Soul on Ice* (1968),[13] George Jackson's *Soledad Brother* (1970), Jarvis Jay Masters' *Finding Freedom: Writings from Death Row* (1997), and Mumia Abu-Jamal's writings, for instance, illuminate only their authors' prison experience and examine this experience through the sensibility of an inmate. These narratives are often fragmented because the authors may not have consciously undertaken the task of writing an autobiography, but rather prison writings may have been collected later and edited into works focusing on their prison experiences. The missing narratives of the childhood and the life after the prison seem to point out that the life in prison, in fact, is a separate lifetime in its own right and therefore worthy of a separate autobiographical work.[14]

Another feature distinguishing prison autobiographies as a genre is that they are often mediated or "collaborative,"[15] a feature that raises questions about authenticity and authorial control. Frequently, the discursive situations and production procedures of prison autobiographies are obscure. Often prisoners have little if any access to writing materials and, therefore, to get their stories published, must rely on the help of people on the outside who listen to their oral narratives, take notes, tape stories, or edit writings submitted to them as private correspondence. What is usually not known is how much these "ghost-writers" control the narratives of prison writers seeking to control and change their public images. Malcolm X's autobiography, written by Alex Haley and published after Malcolm X's assassination, is probably the most well known example of a collaborative prison autobiography, the authorial control of which is not clear.

Tom Cahill, president of Stop Prisoner Rape, Inc. the organization that maintains and edits the *Stop Prisoner Rape* website, offers yet another perspective when he notes that he has to reject some prisoners' letters simply because they are unreadable—either because of illegible handwriting or because "many prisoners who write to [them] are barely literate." Cahill also addresses the question of authenticity, noting that in the case of male-male prison rape he does not suspect many "fraudulent claims" because rape is such a humiliating experience, "especially for heterosexual males who are in the majority of victims."

The questions of authorial control and reliability are also features that link prison autobiographies to slave narratives. As noted above, prison autobiographies, like slave narratives, are often authenticated by persons with established reputations, and prison autobiographies by African American men focus on the affirmation of humanity and manhood in the same manner as slave narratives. Slave narratives not only provide a model for the African American prison autobiography in the sense that they are part of the same African American discursive tradition,[16] but also in the sense that they express a similar urgency for their authors' humanity to be recognized. This fundamental recognition constitutes a starting point for prison reform, both from the point of view of prison as an institution and the point of view of the imprisoned individual.

To facilitate this recognition of humanity to take place, prison autobiographers demystify the experience of imprisonment by simultaneously individualizing it and showing that the experience that they narrate is a representative one. Frederick Douglass, in the letter prefacing *My Bondage and My Freedom* (1855), expressing his concern that his readers would take his story as an anomaly, emphasizes that, although his autobiographical narrative may be regarded "as exceptional in its character," his reason for writing is "not to illustrate any heroic achievements of a man, but to vindicate a just and beneficent principle, in its application to the whole human family, by letting in the light of *truth upon a system,* esteemed by some as a blessing, and by others as a curse and a crime" (166, my italics).[17] Although African American prison autobiographers are strong individuals, their narratives focus not only on their personal experiences, but also on the experiences of inmates as a group as they criticize the institution of prison as a system that criminalizes black males. Thus, their autobiographies work not only as acts of personal liberation, but also as tools for political activism and social analysis.

Traditionally, African American autobiographical writing structures black manhood against the backdrop of the dominant, white masculinity.[18] In prison autobiographies, whiteness represents white masculinity both as a physical male presence and as a system of white patriarchal power that criminalizes black masculinity. Nathan McCall opens *Makes Me Wanna Holler: A Young Black Man in America* (1994) with a primal-scene in which McCall and his "homies" beat up a white boy who ended up in the wrong neighborhood (3). By opening with this episode, McCall locates racism as a major subject of his autobiography, and revenge—or "getback"—as the strategy for dealing with it (4). Another, conflicting strategy for getting even with the "establishment" is his ongoing struggle to *adapt* to the "white mainstream." Although McCall retains some of the political activism-oriented approach of the 1960s and 70s wave of prison autobiographies, his struggle to adapt to the mainstream is a very personal one, as is his struggle with his sexual identity.

At the same time that McCall establishes violent confrontations with whiteness as a defining factor of black manhood, he establishes his own position as an outside observer of the concept of African American masculinity that he outlines. By framing his narrative with assertions such as, "[i]t's hard for me now to believe I was once very much a part of that world," he breaks away from expressions of masculinity that he now holds to be mistaken (414). His childhood and young adulthood experiences consisted of "macho games" such as gang rapes, drugs, gang wars, and breaking-and-enterings (42). Particularly after having gained interest in studying while in prison, McCall assures his readers that he feels removed from the life of his homies even though he is still serving time with them. McCall's transition from a physical macho-masculinity into a more intellectually-oriented manhood is also marked by the replacement of black criminal-hero icons like the characters in the films, *Superfly* and *The Mack,* with prison philosophers and teachers as ideal symbols of black manhood (102, 105).

McCall's assertion that he is now narrating a story about somebody he no longer is both repudiates his criminally violent past as a transitional period of his life and simultaneously lays a foundation for the notion of the temporal sense of his autobiographical self. He further detaches himself from the subject of his narrative by treating the documents recording his crimes as textualized remnants of a past that seem to describe the actions of somebody else (260). These discursive strategies allow McCall to narrate his past without hero-worshipping criminal behavior, and at the same time create a space in which to celebrate his subjectivity as the improved man.

Prison forms the core of McCall's book on two levels. First, although he only spent four years of his life in prison, his prison sentence and the difficulty of overcoming the label of being a criminal informs the narrative of his life up to the time when he finished his book. McCall was 39 years old when his autobiography was published in 1994. Part One of the autobiography depicts his life as a succession of events evolving into a movement that leads him into prison. Part Two slows down to examine the prison experience itself. The contemplative nature of this part of the narrative seems to reflect the manner in which time appears to stop and take on a new meaning when one is "doing time." Part Three, then, moves on from the time of his literal release from prison, to his struggle for a metaphoric release because—due to his criminal record—he retains his status as a prisoner long after he has served his sentence. On another level, McCall metaphorically equates life in prison with his experience of life as a black man who feels alienated in a society that he perceives as white; he claims that, for an African American man, "adapting to the white mainstream was a lot like learning to survive in prison" (299).

While McCall foregrounds his intellectual growth as the defining factor of his progress into the kind of manhood he can appreciate, his sexuality and his relationships with women thematically structure his development from a young man who rapes black girls to a father who teaches his son that rape is wrong. He rationalizes his behavior as a rapist by saying that he and his friends hated black girls because blackness was what connected them to these girls, and that they, without realizing it, "hated the hell out of" themselves (50). He also implicitly places part of the blame on the parents of his generation who had not been taught to how communicate with their children in the ways he is now communicating with his son (411). Non-communication about love and affection in sexual relations was also another rule of the macho games that McCall and his male friends used to play: the "object was to 'get the pussy' without giving love. If a guy was able to do that, he won the game," and if he "developed genuine feelings for her, he lost" (42).

McCall concentrates most of his analysis of prison sexuality in one chapter entitled, "Sex." At the beginning of the chapter, he cites an excerpt from his journal that establishes the mode of the discussion. He describes his relationship to sexuality as a daily "battle against sensuality"—as a fight to "obliterate sexual thoughts" (191). Because it is impossible for him to win this battle, imprisonment results in extremely frustrating tension that makes him "dizzy and aggressive and evil" (191). Living with hundreds of other men who feel the same way, he comments, brings new meaning to the warning, "'Watch your back'" (191). Thus, McCall identifies the fight against sexual thoughts and the danger of being involved in unwanted sexual acts as the main components of prison sexuality. As strategies to transform his sexual energy and to alleviate sexual tension, McCall lists writing, weight lifting, and avoiding the sight of women in magazines or on television, although he also describes how he would "caress" himself, fantasizing about "a date" outside of prison (200–201). Since homophobic fears and fantasies form the center of McCall's struggle to maintain his identity as a heterosexual male, he structures his prison sexuality in the manner that Linda Singer outlines in *Erotic Welfare*. McCall struggles to exclude the "homosexual" from his prisoner identity, but the focus on the fears and phobias itself makes homosexuality a key element of his heterosexual self. Focusing on the battle against "sensuality" and "watching his back," instead of safeguarding his heterosexuality, generates homosexual fantasies in the text and produces homosexuality as the locus of his sexual identity.

Although McCall's contemplation of the nature of prison sexuality seems to aim at offering a new, objective perspective on male sexuality in prison, and homosexuality in particular, his conflicting interpretations of homosexuality and gay subjectivity end up generating homophobic discourse instead of a non-homophobic narrative of male prison sexuality. As a result, his seemingly fresh look continues the tradition of the homophobic prison fantasy typical of fictive accounts of life in prison. McCall signals his aim at objectivity by positioning himself as an observer of rather than a participant in sexual acts, and also by pausing to analyze what he has narrated. From a more subjective point of view, McCall suggests that his own notions of homosexuality mature as he becomes more aware of the various modes of male sexuality in prison. In addition, he implies that his sexual identity is solid enough to allow him to be secure in his masculinity and, at the same time, to realize how a male inmate may represent femininity in prison.

McCall structures his discussion of prison sexuality around a series of incidents that seem to propose the logic that, if a heterosexual man is not careful enough and secure enough in his masculinity, he may be "turned" into a homosexual in prison. The first of the incidents that McCall focuses on in "Sex" is an exchange between himself and Feetball, an inmate from his old neighborhood. Feetball's comment about a newcomer in prison looking "just like Wanda Malone" scares McCall "to death" (193). He analyzes Feetball's comment as an outcome of his having spent a long time in prison, which has confused his conception of his sexuality to the extent that he is no longer aware that some men look like women to him (194). The second incident is a rape scene that McCall involuntarily witnesses. The rape victim, Tooty, subsequently becomes somebody's "boy," or, in McCall's conceptual framework, a homosexual. This gang-rape scene lingers as a recurring element in the book, reinforcing the idea that "homosexual" rape is a key element of prisoner sexuality. The third incident that McCall describes is his meeting with Pauline, a man who, at this stage in McCall's prison experience, "looks *just* like a woman" to him (197).

As the logic of this series of events suggests, the main reason that a man becomes a homosexual in prison, according to McCall, is the tendency toward homosexuality that is latent in all, or at least most, men. If a man is not strong enough to resist his "homosexual impulses," other men may "spot" the weakness in him, "no matter how much [they] try to front it off," and turn him into a homosexual (195–196, 198). These inherent homosexual impulses may surface because of the length of the time spent in prison, physical contact—for example when playing basketball—or the way a man looks at another man in the shower room (193). Most importantly, "becoming a homosexual" seems to depend on a person's suggestibility to external pressure.

Tooty is McCall's main example of the role of suggestibility—of the "head-games" that sexual predators play—to change an inmate's sexual identity (191–192). Tooty is easily manipulated and "turned into a homosexual" by other inmates due to his weak sense of his own masculinity; there was "something" in Tooty that made other men start treating him like a woman (195–196). The gang rape, according to McCall, finally turns Tooty into a homosexual. Likewise, Pauline, an openly gay inmate, became "confused" about his sexuality after being molested by his uncle, and thus he was "turned into a homosexual" despite his attempts to resist these impulses (198).

McCall's theory of male prisoners "turning into homosexuals," mainly through external suggestion that they then internalize, is akin to the Foucaultian notion that external mechanisms of control are most successful when they are internalized and reproduced by the object of control. In the context of McCall's autobiography, the sexual predators—the "wolves"— seem to control the sexual identities of prisoners who lack a strong sense of their own masculinity. The mechanisms used by the "wolves" are manipulative verbal and physical practices, including rape, which the object of their control internalizes and ultimately reproduces as their "punk."

In discussing rape and homosexuality, McCall mixes the concepts of gender and sexual identity to some extent. The rapist who can change the sexual identity of another man is clearly identified as male—or, as McCall puts it, "a guy was even *more* of a man if he could 'flip' another man, turn him into a homosexual" (195). Even though the rapist turns another man into a homosexual, his own sexual identity remains heterosexual.[19] The rape victim, on the other hand, is simultaneously referred to as female and homosexual, which makes "gay" and "female" appear to be synonymous. The interchangeability of "gay" and "female" also is apparent in the way that McCall feminizes Pauline by objectifying his body and stereotyping him as the seductive femme fatale whose "feminine manner" made him "uneasy" (197–198).

These discrepancies between the sexual and gender identities of the rapist and his victim organize homosexual relations through the "sexual role that one plays," as Tomás Almaguer claims. In the context of prison male-male rape, in particular, the "active" and dominant party—the rapist—is considered heterosexual and masculine while his victim, the "passive" and submissive party, is stigmatized as homosexual and feminine. In the case of the rape, however, the situation is obviously different from what Almaguer outlines in his discussion of the tradition of Chicano male-male relations. The rape victim cannot really be said to be "playing a role," but rather is forced into the position of the submissive and feminized party. Almaguer's "scripted" sexual roles are—in the context McCall describes— roles assumed by the rapists and imposed on the victims. Therefore, while the rapist displays his masculine power and dominance, the "submission" of the victim cannot be considered an actual participant in the role-play.

McCall's discursive and conceptual mixing of sexual and gender cate- gories also brings the ideologies of sexual difference and male dominance into a space of seeming gender and sexual sameness. By so doing, McCall's narrative produces the system of heterosexuality in prison in the manner that Kaja Silverman conceptualizes as adherence to the "dominant fic- tion"—the ideology of the stability of heterosexuality and family (15–51). Within the framework of the fiction of male dominance in sexual exchange, homosexual rape in prison represents a *heterosexual* act establishing local social and gender hierarchy and signifying the rapist's hyper-masculinity and power over the feminized victim. McCall's contradictory notion of what constitutes "homosexuality" also promotes the ideology of the stabil- ity of heterosexuality. According to McCall's analysis of prison sexuality, the potential for homosexual behavior is organic to masculinity and can be triggered in an imprisoned male through external manipulation. Yet, fore- grounding the idea that a man may *become* homosexual in prison if he can- not resist the homosexual impulses stimulated by the time spent in prison or by physical contact with other men enables McCall to suggest that het- erosexuality is the essence of male sexuality. In his sex-gender system, in a homosocial space like prison homosexuality exists only temporarily.

Other prison autobiographies and studies of prison experience often emphasize the temporary nature of male-male sexual relations by focusing on the fact that prisoners return to their heterosexual identities after release from prison. The author of "The Story of a Black Punk," for example, nar- rates his guilt and fear about losing his "male identity" as a result of homo- sexual relations in prison, but he also tells how he overcomes these problems with the support of his wife (4). C. Paul Phelps, deputy director of the Louisiana Department of Corrections, also claims that the men habitually practicing homosexual acts in prison are "not medically or clini- cally homosexual. Many resume normal heterosexual relationships when they're released from the institution" (Rideau 43, 85).

The notion that prisoners can alternate between heterosexual and homosexual identities, however, might also indicate that the *sameness* of, rather than the difference between, heterosexuality and homosexuality becomes evident in an environment such as prison.[20] McCall and other African American prison autobiographers do not take this approach, perhaps because to do so would undermine their goal of challenging representations of black masculinity in prison. At a time when an increasing number of African American men spend time in jail or prison, addressing the problem of prison masculinity has become part of the larger project of asserting black masculinity in a racist society that has traditionally sought to control and suppress it. Although recent prison autobiographies by African American men refocus the struggle for black manhood by discussing the question of sexuality from a highly personal point of view, they still retain the traditional ideology of black masculinity as hyper-masculinity and, therefore, continue homophobic discursive practices that critics have noted to be particularly pervasive in African American culture.[21]

McCall repeatedly states that both homosexuality in prison and the danger of becoming gay frighten him. Rather than giving in to the "impulses" within him, he boosts his sexual identity and masculine image by demonstrating his ability to successfully fight his homosexual tendencies in order to fight his fear. Maintaining the notion of heterosexual masculinity necessitates maintaining the notion of male dominance and sexual difference in prison. For this reason, McCall promotes the model of heterosexual masculinity, and simultaneously generates another typically homophobic narrative about male sexuality in prison. McCall acknowledges the existence of consensual male-male sex in prison by mentioning that there were "lots of closeted and openly gay guys" in prison (197). He also points out that "mating rites" among male prisoners were "the most natural thing in the world" for veteran inmates—but not for him (197). A specific discussion of consensual sex remains outside of the realm of McCall's narrative, apparently because it is not part of his personal experience.

A rare prison autobiography by a correctional officer, Ted Conover's *Newjack: Guarding Sing Sing* (2000), takes a different perspective on prison sexuality by claiming that next to "autoeroticism," consensual sex is most common in prisons (262). Conover also points out that in fictive representations of prison life—even in "the supposedly hyperrealistic TV prison series such as *Oz*"—forcible sex is more prevalent because it is "such a fixture of how middle-class America thinks about prison" (262). Like other autobiographers, Conover addresses the question of homosexual relations in prison from an observer's perspective. He is an outsider to his narrative at several levels: first, he is not one of the prisoners he discusses, and thus he is not a participant in the sex acts; second, as a journalist who temporarily became a correctional officer for the purpose of studying prison life, he has no strong personal investment.

Because prison autobiographies exclude consensual male-male sex and include the narrative excess of homosexual rape represented as heterosexual, they simultaneously exclude homosexuality as a perversion and produce it as a fetishized object of fascination in the manner in which Linda Singer theorizes the "outside" as both excluded from the "inside" and as produced by it. Since rape is the primary representation of homosexuality in prison, homosexuality itself is depicted as essentially criminal. The websites, *Stop Prisoner Rape* and the *Human Rights Watch* sponsored "No Escape: Male Rape in U.S. Prisons," which promote public discussion of prison rape, are forums that make the voices of rape victims heard. The authorial anonymity that these websites can provide ensures virtual freedom from self-censorship, and therefore these authors' texts—with explicit language and descriptions of sexual acts—often read like pornography. This tendency is likely to destabilize what Lejeune terms the "pact" between the autobiographer and the reader. If readers perceive the genre of a text as pornography, they are apt to interpret the author's factual narrative as fictive. Read as porn, narratives of prison rape reinforce the author's position as an object of voyeuristic gratification, and generate unintended interpretations of the meanings of the autobiographical texts.

Sociological studies also reinforce the notion of prison homosexual contacts as perversion or a crime in which the rapist is the "real" man and the victim a feminized object who has voluntarily "given up his status as a man" (Rideau 83, 94). Wilbert Rideau and Ron Wikberg's award-winning study, *Life Sentences: Rage and Survival Behind Bars* (1992), cites experts in criminology and psychology,[22] but both Rideau and Wikberg are prisoners in Louisiana State Penitentiary in Angola, the institution which is the focus of the study, so, even though the book is not directly autobiographical, it narrates its editors' experiences. Like McCall's autobiography, *Life Sentences* implies that rape is the main manner of asserting one's masculinity in prison, although *Life Sentences* uses a more direct narrative method, stating, for instance, that "there are very few ways in prison for a man to show how powerful he is—and the best way to do so is for one to have a slave, another who is in total submission to him" (75). The institutional control that denies assertions of masculinity by criminalizing male-male sex in prison simultaneously produces rape as *the* means to assert male domination.[23] In other words, the same-sex rape that affirms the masculinity of the rapist, while feminizing the victim, makes the act of rape a method for the rapist to assert his masculinity within a system that is largely based on stripping prisoners of any means of affirming their masculinity.

The homophobic "epidemic condition"—to apply Linda Singer's terminology—used to rationalize the control of same-sex relations in prison seems to hold that, unless a penal institution criminalizes homosexual activity, it in fact encourages it because homosexuality is seen as "contagious," in the sense that McCall's logic of time, physical contact, and the mind suggests. The AIDS scare has, in part, reinforced this "panic logic." Therefore, in order to prevent American prisons from becoming generators of homosexuality, all sexual activity has been criminalized.

The actual administrative control in prisons, however, seems to both exclude homosexuality and produce what it supposedly controls. The prison administration excludes homosexuality by being reluctant to document and punish the same-sex rape that it euphemistically refers to as "the homosexual problem" (Rideau 74). In fact, while aware that rape is a severe problem in prisons, these institutions use rape as a way to control the prison population (Rideau 89–90). Studies show that prison officials ignore rape since they perceive aggressive prisoners to be more cooperative with prison authority when they are allowed to continue their abuse of "weaker" prisoners (Rideau 94, 101).[24] Ironically, the only prisoners who are "protected" from homosexual contacts are gay men (Rideau 95). Gay men are often segregated from the general prison population because they are either thought to create aggressive rivalries or because as "effeminate men" they are projected to be potential rape victims (Rideau 101–102).

On a discursive level, the regulatory practice of prohibiting male-male sex in prison produces the narrative excess of rape in prison autobiography, since rape is the primary context in which an autobiographer can analyze his masculinity. However, a narrative that excludes homosexuality by representing homosexual rape as a heterosexual act, and that involves only the rapist, the victim, and the disinterested observer, makes it difficult for the prison autobiographer to find the discursive space to fully analyze his sexual identity. Thus, his autobiographical self remains incomplete. Autobiographers such as Nathan McCall negotiate this space by detaching themselves from their narratives of rape in order to locate their masculinity outside of the context of homosexuality that feminizes them and, therefore, excludes them. Several rap artists who narrate their prison experiences in the explicit mode of gangsta rap also stay within the detached observer's position; the prisoner whose "cellmate's raped on the norm,/ And passed around the dorm, you can hear his asshole getting torn" only reports what happens around him, not *to* him (2Pac).[25]

The "real man" tends to remain a mythical absent figure in prison autobiographical writing, since nobody seems to want to claim the subjectivity of the rapist.[26] What works as an assertion of masculinity in a real-life prison situation does not lend itself to public scrutiny as an autobiographical narrative, even an anonymous one. Since the subjectivity of the rapist is not desired, Almaguer's theory of dominant and submissive participants in male-male sexual relationships does not seem to apply to prison rape. The rapist may be able to locally and temporarily boost his masculinity as the dominant and active one, but will not do so after having left the prison's homosocial and discursive space.

Sanyika Shakur, in *Monster: The Autobiography of an L.A. Gang Member* (1993), implicitly represents the rapist as his *Doppelgänger* through describing himself as "the silent observer" of what seemed to develop into a rape scene (303). By allowing Fat Rat to humiliate and assault another cellmate in his presence, Shakur—a.k.a. "Monster" Kody—asserts the sameness of his own sexual identity and the would-be rapist, rather than identifying with the victim, B.T., who by submitting "had yielded his manhood" (294). Shakur further demonstrates his masculinity by convincing Fat Rat not to rape B.T. because he himself "ain't into that shit" (302). Thus, he asserts his masculinity both by indirectly claiming the position of the rapist—by being an accomplice to the ripping of B.T.'s manhood—and by becoming his savior by not letting the rape take place.

The only rapists in prison autobiographies are either rape victims who become rapists after their release from prison or men like Nathan McCall who affirm their subjectivity as rapists, but only outside of the context of prison. Some authors also narrate the experiences of becoming rapists or murderers after their release as a result of the abuse they suffered in prison. Michael Robtoy, for example, describes how he, after his release from juvenile hall, went on a "'homophobic crime spree,' beating and robbing gay men in an attempt, he says, to regain his manhood" (Harris, "Aftershock"). His crime spree culminated in murder (Harris, "Aftershock"). This discursive mode, instead of providing the space for the rapist to examine his sexuality, demonizes the rape victim as a "time bomb" ready to explode and re-implicates homosexuality as a crime.

Nathan McCall identifies himself as a rapist when he describes his life during his early teens and young adulthood. Gang rapes—or "running trains"—on young black girls are a theme in his autobiographical struggle to understand and redefine black male sexuality. He rationalizes his own and his friends' behavior as a misguided assertion of masculinity within the tradition of black manhood; rape was "another way for a guy to show the other fellas how cold and hard he was" (50). In contrast to McCall's analysis of homosexual rape in prison from the standpoint of an outside observer, he describes himself as a participant in rape scenes that take place in heterosexual contexts. Heterosexual rape affirms his inclusion in the realm of masculinity, while homosexual rape would exclude him from it by implicating his sexual identity as feminized.

McCall's narrative juxtaposes Shirley, the woman he raped as a young adult, and Tooty, the man who was gang-raped in prison. In a way, Tooty and Shirley's identities as rape victims become fused in the narrative, and McCall's analysis of Shirley and his other female rape victims functions to continue his discussion of prison rape. By juxtaposing female and male rape victims, McCall marks the sexual identity of Tooty and other male-male rape victims as feminized, while his own identity remains masculine and heterosexual.

Although McCall claims that one the reasons why he wants to ana-lyze his life is to understand women and "to free [himself] from sexism that had led [him] to be so abusive toward women before," his confessional mode produces sexist narrative that polarizes black manhood and black womanhood (250). He objectifies black women by giving them no voice of their own and by analyzing them as if their minds were a continuation of his own introspective contemplation. When discussing his identity as a rapist, for example, McCall psychoanalyzes Shirley as one whose identity has been destroyed by the "shame" of being a victim of multiple gang rapes (241). The only word McCall reports as Shirley's own is her response, "Fine," to his question of how she is (241).[27]

McCall also puts prison rape into a larger social and cultural context by using rape as a metaphor for discussing mental violence and racism in the workplace. By using rape as a metaphoric device and by looking at him-self as a rapist in the manner that makes it only *his* concern, not his vic-tim's, McCall dilutes the notion of rape as a violent crime, and as a result alleviates some of the guilt of being a rapist himself. He uses rape, for example, to describe how his female co-worker becomes convinced of her inferiority after people at the work place use manipulative techniques that are similar to the ones male prisoners used to turn Tooty into a homosexual (329). McCall himself also feels violated by the racist gazes of his co-work-ers in the predominantly white workplace and those gazes remind him of the "predatory gazes" that he saw in prison (257).

Black-white sexual relationships are not an issue discussed in terms other than metaphoric rape in McCall's autobiography. The closest he comes to discussing interracial sexual relationships are his brief remarks about how white males in restrooms had to see "if the myths about black men's penis size were true," and how white women were "viewed as the ultimate catch" when he was young (300, 42). The omission of interracial sex is glaring, since McCall distinctly analyzes his manhood in the context of his struggle against the white mainstream—after all, the identity of black men as rapists has been an American cultural fantasy since slavery, and in the imagery of the majority of prison rape narratives the black man is the aggressor.

Although McCall claims that prison is the "one place in America where black men rule," he avoids marking black men as rulers of prison by assigning them the subjectivity of the rapist, and particularly not of the rapist of white men (149). In most of McCall's narrative, people other than black men are hardly mentioned, so it therefore seems that all the participants in rapes are black. It seems that erases the image of black male as a rapist by selectively removing "race" from the context of his narrative of prison rape and by representing himself as a man who does not participate in male-male rape. Being a rapist is something McCall has put behind him, and his fight with the white male mainstream does not involve sexuality; therefore his masculinity is not located in the fantasy of the black man raping the white woman either.[28]

Sanyika Shakur, on the contrary, fantasizes about male-male rape in his narrative and even situates himself at the very locus of the rape. As a result, he not only provides his readers the pleasure of the rape fantasy, but also offers a kind of absolution from the guilty pleasure because the rape does not actually take place. In addition to offering himself and his audience the rush of expecting the violent sexual act, Shakur represents himself as the "good guy" in the scene; his rather passive resistance to the beating and humiliation of B.T., and his unwillingness to participate in a gang rape makes him into the hero who saves the already feminized victim.

African American prison autobiographers "poach on" cultural representations of black masculinity by refusing to be excluded from contemporary discourse as illiterate criminals. The project of redefining black male identity is particularly important for African American prison autobiographers in the cultural climate in which black manhood is typically represented and fetishized as corporeal and as inferior to white masculinity. African American prison autobiographers use sexuality—and the male-male prison rape, in particular—both as a central theme for redefining black masculinity and as a *tactical vehicle* for aggressively seeking the attention of their potential audiences, both in the high culture realm of literature and in the popular discourse of rap. Thus, the authors are "tacticians," in de Certeau's sense of the term, because they resist the "strategic" or institutionalized representational power and actively utilize cracks within that representational framework for their resistance.

For African American prison autobiographers, the project of redefining black masculinity through focusing on sexuality creates problems that they typically solve by detaching themselves from their narrative space. Although the rapist is regarded as the "real man" in the context of male-male prison rape because the victim is seen as feminized, African American authors "vigilantly" resist the traditional representation of the black male as a rapist. Since rape is also regarded as a mechanism that has the capacity to redefine prisoner sexuality—to change one's sexual identity from masculine and heterosexual to feminine and homosexual—prison autobiographers do not assume the subjectivity of the rapist because to do so would put them in the position of being a participant in a homosexual exchange. By taking this stance, the authors also promote the notion of rape as a sexual act, not merely as an assertion of masculine power.

In addition to detaching themselves from the narrative locus of male-male rape, African American prison autobiographers produce the system of heterosexuality as the model for structuring sexual hierarchies in prison. To accomplish this, the authors use traditionally heterosexualist measures—such as representing the other as feminized—to assert male dominance in the discursive space and real-life context of prison in which male agency is practically obliterated. Although the aim of the prison autobiographers seems to be to avert the public gaze away from the issue of homosexuality, the narrative strategy of detaching themselves from scenes that would implicate homosexuality, however, ends up highlighting homosexual tension rather than eliminating it. This tension, then, generates and reinforces homophobic notions in the context of male-male relations in prison.

The concerns of autobiographers reflected in their convoluted narrative treatments of sexuality also foreground the complexity of the instability, or provisionality, of prison sexual identity itself. The idea that homosexual rape—or just male gazes on male bodies—can change one's sexual identity is particularly prevalent in prison narratives, and highlights the instability of prison sexuality. The notion of the unstable prison sexuality becomes even more complicated when considering that victims of prison rape can become "homosexual" serial rapists themselves. The fantasy of prison rape culture is thus also reproduced outside prison narratives in the image of the rape victim as a "time bomb" about to explode in our midst.

Institutional reluctance to officially address the problem of prison rape also feeds the fantasy of the violence and perversity of prison sexuality. The reluctance to punish sexual predators seems to work as a protective method within the institution itself: in order to prevent violent impulses from being redirected towards correctional officers, institutional policies often simply deny the existence of prison rape, or dismiss the problem—expressing a "boys-will-be-boys attitude" or by labeling rape a "homosexual problem"—and by doing so, abdicate all institutional responsibility because homosexual sex acts are prohibited in the prison. Institutional prison narratives remain unready to address the problem of rape or talk about homosocial prison sexuality in the explicit manner the media and the prison autobiographers already do.

Chapter Three

Divide and Conquer: Racialized Hierarchies in the Contemporary Prison Novel

In *Going Up the River: Travels in a Prison Nation* (2001), Joseph Hallinan discusses the American prison industry as a seemingly unstoppable power that shapes nation through the "merger of punishment and profit" (xi). During his journey, Hallinan contemplates the locations of modern prisons and touches upon the social hierarchies of race and class that the system of imprisonment reflects and reproduces. Most new prisons are located in remote rural areas that are also the "whitest places in America" (209). While most of the correctional officers employed by these institutions are white and rural, most inmates are black and urban (xiii, 209). One of the examples Hallinan cites is the Terrel Unit in Polk County, Texas, where 75 percent of the guards are white and 83 percent of the prisoners are non-white (87). A major reason why rural "white" locations are prioritized is the availability of a white labor pool that is preferred by prison administrators "almost universally" (85). In these rural locations white guards are perceived to be "unsympathetic, or even antipathetic, to the aspirations, life styles and ethnic values of the [non-white] prisoners" (84).[1] While other scholars have pointed out that race is an issue at every stage of the U.S. criminal justice system,[2] Hallinan's observations suggest that the system of imprisonment is racially polarized as early as the time when sites for new prison facilities are chosen.

This chapter focuses on how the discourse of the contemporary prison novel challenges socio-historical and ideological notions about racialized hierarchies in prison. In it I consider what race means in the discursive practice of prison policies, how the social structure of prisons is racially organized, and how the prison novel acts as a counter-discourse to these notions of meaning and structure.

First of all, I argue that contemporary prison novels suggest that the racial organization that prisons use to prevent and correct racial conflicts in fact generates them. Thus, the racialized hierarchies, in part, create surges of violence that are presumed to be inherent to prison life.[3] Second, I argue that—and as a result of the above—the racialized hierarchies of prisons not only reflect the racial hierarchies of American society but create hierarchies of their own kind, hierarchies that, for example, support the cultural fantasy that holds that prison is "the one place in America that black men rule" (McCall 151). In this context, I discuss how gangs function as a discursive tool for rationalizing the racial organization of prison policies. Third, I argue that these hierarchies also racialize the identities of prisoners, and as a result deny them their individual identities. This identification through race is another aspect of prison policy that contemporary prison novels challenge.

The architecture of prisons represents the ideology that order can be created and maintained by the careful classification and placement of prisoners.[4] Each unit of prison architecture—each block, tier, and cell—is used to house different kinds of prisoners, categorized by the kinds of crimes they committed, the length of their sentences, and the inmates' sexuality: there are separate units for murderers and for prisoners who committed nonviolent crimes, for prisoners serving short-term sentences and for prisoners serving life or death sentences, and for heterosexual prisoners and homosexual prisoners. The distribution of jobs, when jobs are available, also creates class system where good behavior is rewarded by jobs with a better pay and more comfortable working environments.[5]

Contemporary prison novels demonstrate, however, that the ideology of racial organization permeates other dimensions of the logic of order and imprisonment.[6] The architectural solutions that separate prisoners into homogenous sections and manageable units only represent the surface structure of the hierarchical organization of the prison, while the socio-historical and ideological notions of racialized hierarchies are represented in its deep structure. Following the logic that prisoners need to be racially segregated in order to avoid racial conflicts, within the units primarily organized by the inmates' criminal records, prisoners are also reorganized racially. These unofficial racialized hierarchies—and their use as a manipulative method in the institutional discourse—become visible in the discourse of contemporary prison novel.[7]

In Chapter One I discussed race and masculinity from the point of view of white heroship in futuristic prison films and in Chapter Two from the point of view of representations of prison sexuality in African American prison autobiography. In this chapter I draw on Michael Omi and Howard Winant's definition of race in *Racial Formation in the United States* (1994) as a "concept that signifies and symbolizes social conflicts and interests" and the meanings of which are "constantly being transformed by political struggle" (55). The discourse of race plays a fundamental role in structuring and representing the social hierarchies in prison narratives, and the contemporary prison novel as a genre questions and rewrites perceived notions of how these racialized hierarchies represent prison life. The prison novel thus works as a counter-narrative to the institutional discourse of prison policies, and also the discourse of the media, which—according to prison fiction—supports the institutional discourse.

By making racialized hierarchies visible, the prison novel contests the image of imprisonment represented, in particular, in the visual media—television and prison film—in which the body of the prisoner serves as the locus of racial representation. While the visual image in the media racializes criminality by associating the criminal body with the criminal act, the prison novel questions the seeming transparency of racialized criminality by focusing on the institutional hierarchies that participate in creating that image. Thus, the prison novel represents the modernist project of making race visible in literature, while it simultaneously questions the methods of racial visibility within the realm of prison discourse in general. The prison novel's commitment to telling its own "truth" in terms of structural injustice reflects the kind of critical stance that Robyn Wiegman calls for in *American Anatomies* (2–4).[8] By focusing on the social hierarchies of race in prison, the prison novel averts the critical gaze from the body of the criminal to the task of uncovering the ideological configurations of the racial dynamics that shape the discourse of imprisonment.

As fiction that aims at uncovering some "truth" about imprisonment the prison novel represents "political" fiction in the sense that it is literature that exposes the racial-political nature of prison policies typically perceived either as nonpolitical or as practical necessities for prison management—issues that would otherwise remain embedded in the institution-originated discourse.[9] Some prison novels overtly acknowledge the political nature of their narratives, as does Nathan C. Heard's *House of Slammers* (1983), the main primary text examined in this chapter. In his novel, Heard presents a compelling case for how prison administrations use the divide-and-conquer technique to manipulate the racialized balance of power in prison. Likewise, Edward Bunker's novel *The Animal Factory*

(1977) represents how the prison administration manages inmates by reinforcing the racial divisions between them.

Another of Bunker's prison novels, *Dog Eat Dog* (1996), on the other hand, displays a less conscious questioning of race as an organizing element in the social hierarchies of prison, although it does focus on it. For example, the narrator of *Dog Eat Dog* describes the morning recreation on the yard of a California juvenile institution in the following way: "The neat ranks disintegrated and formed clusters by race. Chicanos were half the total, fifteen, followed by nine blacks, five whites, and a pair of half-brothers, one of whom was Vietnamese while his half-brother was a quarter Native American, a quarter black and half Vietnamese" (2). Although the novel opens with this disinterested recognition of the racial composition of the institution,[10] later in the text the narrator presents a more critical view of the use of interracial conflicts to cover up corrections-officer brutality: when Troy Cameron, one of the white inmates, is assaulted by the staff, the staff incriminate black inmates, stating that Cameron "was jumped by some niggers in the tank" (218). Thus, *Dog Eat Dog* combines the narrative modes of treating racialized criminality as transparent—by identifying Chicanos and blacks as the majority of the inmates, for example—and of critiquing the use of the supposed racial conflicts between inmates to cover up real conflicts between correctional officers and inmates.

Because most authors of prison fiction became professional writers during or soon after their incarceration, prison novels often are autobiographical in nature and narrated from the prisoner's point of view. Chester Himes, author of the novel *Cast the First Stone* (1952), is probably the most well known pioneer of American prison fiction with serious literary merit. Like Himes, other prominent authors of prison novels such as Malcolm Braly, Edward Bunker, and Nathan Heard started their writing careers in prison. Some exceptions to the male inmates' domination of the genre of prison fiction are Dorothy Bryant, whose novel *Prisoners* (1980) depicts the relationship between a middle-class female activist and a male prisoner, Ernest Brawley, whose novel *The Rap* (1974) is based on his experience as a former correctional officer, and Stephen King, whose novella "Rita Hayworth and the Shawshank Redemption" (1982) and serial novel *The Green Mile* (1996) are influenced by other prison narratives rather than based on his own experience.

Prison novels can be characterized as "institutional novels" because the prison as institution dominates the narrative to such a degree that the institution itself constitutes a hero[11] and because the institution characteristically is the focus of severe critique in the novels. Donald Goines' *White*

Man's Justice, Black Man's Grief (1973), for instance, claims to reveal "the bigotry built into our [prison] system" through its focus on the bail bond system, which leaves poor Americans unnecessarily in jails and prisons because they cannot afford the bond (front cover, 7–8). Prisons are criticized in the prison novel to such an extreme degree that the future of the institution is seen to be in danger. Jerome Washington writes, in *Iron House: Stories from the Yard* (1994), that prison writers "are often called liars and troublemakers by the officials" and that the "most effective writers are slandered as terrorists who plan to overthrow the warden's administration," with the result that their writings are banned and their writing materials confiscated (Preface).

As fiction critiquing the conditions of the prison as an institution, prison novels also represent the literary tradition of realism, or even naturalism, with their "blunt styles [that] portray individuals chewed up by the system, which somewhat mindlessly muddles along no matter what occurs" (Massey 7). To emphasize the realistic nature of the narratives, prison novels—like prison autobiographies—are often authenticated as true stories by the authors themselves or by other prominent figures. Some critics even make the essentialist claim that authentic prison fiction can only be written by authors who have first hand knowledge of life in prison: prison is "a place so corrupt and violent, populated by human beings so grotesquely and unpredictably different from you and me, that its appalling contours and the behavior of its denizens can be portrayed only by a writer who has been there" (Styron, "Introduction" to *Dog Eat Dog*, viii).

Perhaps the reason why prison fiction is less popular than prison film is its position in between genres.[12] Prison novels are fictive narratives of prison life, yet they are perceived to be factual, or at least fact-based, due to their autobiographical and realist nature, and due to their political aim of revealing the truth about the system of imprisonment.[13] As a category that is a cross between fact and fiction, and between serious and entertaining literature, prison fiction is only now being recognized as a genre of its own in critical reviews and in publishers' and book sellers' publications. Prison novels often become known only after they have been made into major motion pictures like Malcolm Braly's *On the Yard* (1967), Edward Bunker's *The Animal Factory* (1977), and Stephen King's *The Green Mile* (1996).

The popularity of prison films such as those noted above has made audiences more receptive to prison fiction as well. As a result, throughout the 1990s an increasing number of more prison novels have been published. The public's tendency to perceive prison fiction as equivalent to the genres of autobiography and "true crime" fiction, on the one hand, and to the genre of "action" film, on the other, may have a dual effect on the manner in which readers interpret its meanings. Read as true-crime narratives, prison novels are likely to reach their aim of raising public awareness of the conditions of prisons and the racism embedded in them. Transformed into action films with scenes valorizing and sensationalizing individual heroic performances, however, the prison novel often loses some of its critical edge.

Nathan C. Heard's novel, *House of Slammers* (1983), is set in the New Jersey State Penitentiary at Trenton, where the author himself spent twelve years (Massey 183). The main thematic focus of the novel is the unification of prisoners for a work strike in an attempt to change some of the conditions in the prison. The protagonist of the novel, William "Beans" Butler, unites the prison population behind a list of grievances agreed upon by the leaders of the various cliques of the prisoners. This strategic organization of prisoners beyond racial lines and personal disagreements has severe and unwanted repercussions, however. From the point of view of the prison administration and the ensuing media coverage, the strike escalates into a race riot and, as a result, ends up in a massacre of its leaders. The organization of prisoners is ultimately unstable due to the lack of loyalty between inmates and the changes that the strikers accomplish are disappointingly minimal. As a vehicle of counter-discourse, *House of Slammers* focuses on the theme of prisoner organization in order to uncover how prison administrations control inmate populations by manipulating the racialized institutional discourse. Yet, the novel concludes that even an organized and united prison population has little influence in effecting changes in its own living conditions.

Gangs epitomize the racial organization of the prison in prison narratives, and racialized gangs are also what Heard uses to introduce his main characters in *House of Slammers*. The two main racial groups represented in Trenton are African Americans and whites. The African American prisoners follow the leaderships of two central characters: the black Muslims are led by Mustafa Abdul-Haqq (formerly Marcus Early) and the black Nationalists by Wally Allen. The white prison population also falls into two factions. Casey Ryan heads the group of neo-Nazis, which he organized because, as he puts it, "white inmates didn't have enough strong representation in the penal system" (15). Joe Valli, another white inmate, leads men who hope to gain from his organized-crime connections when they get out of prison (32). Besides these four major groups, whose leaders participate in the strike negotiations, there are two minor groups: the Puerto Rican Nationalists and a clique of whites who do not wish to be associated with either the Mafia or the Nazis.

The administrative and correctional staff of the institution is divided into two groups, but these groups are not race based, since the majority of the staff is white. Warden Sharp, with his "penology conference knowledge," represents the new liberal school of prison administration while Chief Deputy Rangler represents the old-school belief in discipline and punishment. Rangler illustrates his ideology of prison management by asserting that, to earn respect among prisoners, "you don't negotiate, you manipulate" (120). Most correctional officers follow his advice. Only one of the two black officers identified in the novel is said to represent a "new breed of black officers" whose attitude toward authority resembles the attitude of the inmates—Officer Pilgrim questions the rules and regulations of the institution too much to be trusted by officers of the old school (49).

Although the main inmate characters in the novel are identified as representatives of racially segregated gangs, the narrative of *House of Slammers* demonstrates that this racial organization—typically used to normalize and rationalize the racial structure of prisons in prison narratives—can be transcended by strategically unifying the inmates around a common cause. Beans Butler works as the neutral mediator between the leaders of the groups, although, as an African American, he is perceived, particularly by non-black prisoners, to represent blacks.

Most of the novel is narrated through the consciousness of Butler, and since he does not personally share the religious or ideological beliefs of his fellow inmates, the critique of gang affiliation is presented through his eyes. According to Butler, black Nationalism is "a dead issue in America" and "its graveyard [is] the prisons where men of no actual commitment to real political issues" rehearse the rhetoric of the movement, but—without real knowledge of its meaning—do not produce change within the prison population and even end up making their own positions worse by offering themselves as targets for correctional discipline (103). Black Muslims, on the other hand, lost the essence of their ideology at the moment when white people, or "the devil," were allowed to join the Nation of Islam (236).

The racial segregation that the narrative first acknowledges by introducing the main characters through their gang affiliations is also undercut by its focus on aspects of the prisoners' identities that are not related to their gang based racialized identities. For example, the friendship between Casey Ryan, the leading white supremacist, and Willie "Lump-Lump" Moore, the black "village idiot" of the prison, illustrates how the narrative in *House of Slammers* counters institutional racialized identities. Although Ryan may be motivated by a special kind of enjoyment in having a black man provide him sexual pleasures, nevertheless their relationship is a close one and difficult for his followers to understand (30–31). The only serious conflict in which Ryan is involved is the killing of a white corrections officer who had an affair with his wife while he was incarcerated. Although the murder reinforces his identity as a hardened criminal, his character is represented through his role as a jealous husband and his friendship with Moore and not primarily through his actions as a neo-Nazi gang leader.

Like the killing of the correctional officer that, in part, defines Ryan's character, other major conflicts in *House of Slammers* are also *not* inspired by interracial hatred. Although they are not racially motivated, the violent events that occur throughout the narrative are typical of prison fiction in that they focus on sex. For example, one inmate is killed as a result of Ryan's jealous rage over "Miss Amber" and a gang rape ends with the suicide of the rape victim. While race based gangs seem to structure the hierarchy of prison society in the novel, other more individual considerations override this representation of prisoners and their relationships with each other.

The ideology of traditional black-white opposition, however, problematizes the seamless unification of the prisoner community. Although both black and white leaders agree to jointly negotiate the list of grievances to be presented to the prison administration, the leaders of the black Muslims and the black Nationalists voice concerns about acting "in concert with the devils" (96). Despite the fact that at least 75 percent of the inmates are black, they perceive the system to be white, and believe that the white prisoners "feel the power of the rulers of society vicariously" and think that they are "better than [blacks] because they look like the people who make the decisions" (97).

The black leaders, Mustafa Abdul-Haqq and Wally Allen, believe that the dignity and manhood of the African American male are at stake if they join forces with the white prisoners (99). Allen makes his position clear by stating, *"I'm a man,* man. And I don't need no white folks to lead me *nowhere"* (176). For historical and ideological reasons he is convinced that white male leadership—even in a prisoner population that is predominantly black—threatens the sovereignty of black manhood. In this sense, then, the possibility of racial conflict itself in prison is also unrelated to individual action, but inherent in the racialized nature of the system of imprisonment, which is based on the ideologies of race in American society.

Abdul-Haqq also criticizes some black inmates for losing sight of why they should be unified. Blacks in prison should not unify "around their misery," but against the institution of prison as a "racist- political attempt . . . to keep jails functioning as an industry that provides mostly white people

with a steady paycheck" (233). Abdul-Haqq believes that through a collec-
tive effort there are tangible ways to overcome this "devils' tricknology"
(233). A more local instance of the misplaced boundaries of prisoner politics is the heated discussion concerning whether or not gays should be
allowed to join the work strike. Even Abdul-Haqq, who advocates solidarity among black prisoners and points out the shortsightedness of others in
this regard, refuses to compromise when his religious beliefs concerning
sexuality are at stake; the only group that remains outside of the strike
effort, then, is the gay prisoners (178–181).

Another critical point that Beans Butler makes is that prisons are part
of the capitalist system that excludes and contains African Americans, particularly poor African Americans (196, 200). He claims that the capitalist
system is a rich people's conspiracy through which laws can be changed to
the advantage of the privileged, and that prisons with mostly black and
poor inmates are an extension of that conspiracy (193–194). In this capitalist conspiracy, according to Butler, social changes such as the end of segregation are not genuinely changes toward democratic equality, but forms of
social containment, and as such function in the same manner as cosmetic
changes created by "band-aid" programs within prisons that, rather than
making any significant changes in the lives of prisoners, only hide society's
scabs (196, 200). Therefore, Butler claims, obeying the political, social, and
economical rules of the systems of society and the prison is counter-productive for black prisoners (194).

The prison administration's response to the prisoners' grievances in
House of Slammers demonstrates how "band-aid" solutions are implemented. The demands that the inmates united to express included vocational and educational training, based on the rationale that they will not
always be prisoners and need the training to prepare for their return to
society (98). Instead of considering these options, the prison administration
offers some new sports equipment and an extra movie during the week of
the work strike (184). Although the offer does not meet the demands of the
prisoners, it provides several beneficial outcomes for the prison authority.
First, the concessions make it seem that changes accommodating the strikers have been made, and second, the promise of new sports equipment and
a movie satisfies the less goal-oriented prisoners and, perhaps, alleviates
some of their resentment towards the administration. At the same time, not
upgrading educational and vocational opportunities ensures that prisoners
have little or no recourse for self-betterment, and also works as a method
preventing further prisoner organizing. The institutional strategy of empha-
sizing sports and entertainment instead of education thus produces fewer

inmates like the prison-educated Beans Butler, who has gained an awareness of the prison as a socio-political system that prompts him to organize
other prisoners to strike.

The strategies of the prison administration that most clearly illustrate
its "divide and conquer" method range from efforts to bribe individual
prisoners to physically dividing the prison population into separate groups
without giving a reason. The administration seeks to influence Butler, for
instance, by threatening to revoke his work privileges and the possibility of
a parole hearing (156). By dividing prisoners into two large groups that are
not able to communicate with each other, the administration manipulates
the prisoners into suspecting that the other group is in some way privileged.
The administration also pits the racial gangs against each other by seemingly negotiating with the African American leaders and not with the white
ones, and exploits the rifts between black prisoners representing different
religious and political views. Butler illustrates his disillusionment and
growing pessimism about the possibility of change by commenting that the
method of divide and conquer works particularly "splendidly" in prison,
where the subjects of manipulation are emotionally insecure: hatred and
intolerance between prisoners is easily stirred even when the manipulative
plan is "well-known to its victims"(134).

Despite his pessimism, Butler recognizes signs of positive development
in prison racial relations. He claims, for instance, that since the prison population has become overwhelmingly black "complaints about overt racism
could no longer be shunted aside and ignored" (131). He also believes that
"human rights" for prisoners, who lost their "rights as citizens" when they
were sentenced, can eventually be restored (188). For Butler, the right to
vocational training and educational opportunities in prison is a question of
human rights because the lack of preparation for reentry into society
extends the effect of incarceration into the indefinite future of prisoners.
Butler's optimistic stance is based on his studies of teachings by philosophers "from Buddha to Jesus to Marx to Baraka" who have convinced him
that their common message—that "people are the ultimate power in the
world"—will enable people, including prisoners, to get together to make a
change for all, not just for the privileged few (195).

From the prison administration's point of view, however, the strike—
or the "riot," as they called it—is not a question of human rights but of
maintaining the control of the system of imprisonment and the hierarchies
that support it. In *House of Slammers,* the administrators who believe in
discipline and punishment as the guiding philosophy of prison management
advocate proactive methods of keeping the system in control (123). The

"manipulate, don't negotiate" ideologists perceive both possible and actual conflicts as an opportune means for restoring the equilibrium of the system (121). The possibility of conflicts—the "real *and* imagined threats that convicts represent"—allows them to enforce preventive methods to control the prison population, and actual conflicts such as "riots" enable them to make demands for the "extra manpower and equipment" needed to enact more preventive methods (120–121).

Thus, the ideology of the prison management in *House of Slammers* represents the current political ideology of imprisonment in the United States in microcosm—a logic of discipline and punishment that feeds itself in a circular manner. This logic holds that, because of increased prisoner populations, there is a need for more prison facilities, which in turn means increased prisoner populations, and even more demands for more new prisons. As Heard's novel points out, the prison system and the maintenance of its rules and hierarchies outweighs other considerations regarding inmates whose actions could produce chaos, or an end to the system (159).

In Heard's novel, the administration, by using rhetoric that suggests violent disorder in the system, also manipulates media coverage of the strike in order to support its own aims. First, the prison administrators insist on calling the work strike "a riot" in order to give the impression that the incident is potentially dangerous and chaotic rather than an organized movement. Also, Warden Sharp's statement that a "small number of inmates have become disruptive about unspecified grievances" suggests that the prisoners' demonstration is a spontaneous riot created by a few subversives, and not a strike initiated by a unified prison population with a well-defined list of demands (221). Sharp also reports that the prison administration has reason to believe that the riot "began as a fight between a Nazi-type group and the Black Muslims" (222). Thus, by labeling the riot a "race riot" the prison administration produces a "media event" that is apt to generate more news coverage than would a peaceful strike, and as a result originates discourse that not merely represents the world, but "acts in and upon it" (Fiske 5). By manipulating public discourse in this manner, the administration also sets itself up to take credit for having effectively solved a violent racial conflict, and diverts public attention away from penal problems that are directly related to the performance of the administrators themselves.

This kind of racializing of news covering a prison uprising is described by Theodore Davidson in *Chicano Prisoners: The Key to San Quentin* (1974). He claims that there are unofficial (and often illegal) forms of social control in prison, and, as an example, cites a minor incident involving a black kitchen worker and a guard—an incident that was deliberately allowed to escalate into the "so-called race riots of Wednesday, January 18, 1967 [in San Quentin]"(163–164). According to Davidson, due to various ulterior motives concerning changes in the power and authority relations between the prison's custody and treatment staff, the staff manipulated the prisoners to riot (165–166). Davidson also states that, by calling the incident a "race riot," the prison administrators not only gave the public a false sense of satisfaction—a sense that it understood what the incident was about—but also deflected attention away from its true cause, which would have subjected them to public criticism (168).[14]

References to the Attica riot forms a frame to the novel that contributes to its naturalistic and deterministic narrative mode. After the work strike, the prison management in *House of Slammers* is somewhat concerned with how suspicious the media would be if they eliminated the "leaders" of the "riot" soon after the event took place (242). After discussing how quickly the media, and therefore the public, forgot what happened at Attica, the administrators decide to stage "an escape" that results in the killing of the main prisoner characters (243). At the beginning of the novel, Beans Butler foreshadows the theme of a riot gone awry by lamenting how Attica lives only in its textualized remains—in the "picaresque anthologies featuring convict poetry" (17). At the end of the novel, the administrators' comments reinforce Butler's sense that the legacy of Attica has been lost: prison authorities can still engage in punitive methods that involve eliminating prisoners and use manipulative rhetoric that covers up the administrative problems inside the prison without concerns about legal or ethical repercussions.

By demonstrating how institutional discourse manipulates public perceptions of life in prison, Nathan Heard's *House of Slammers* challenges the cultural fantasy that black inmates control prisons and the notion that social hierarchies in prison are inherently race based. In the institutional discourse, and in the media coverage based on it, a peaceful interracial organization of prisoners is turned into a dangerous riot between warring racial groups. The manner in which the prison authorities establish and manipulate racialized social hierarchies generates racial conflicts rather than preventing them. By individualizing prisoner identities, the novel also represents its prisoner characters as men with concerns that transcend issues directly related to their institutionalized identities, identities that are extensions of their racial identities. The individualizing of prisoner identities does not mean glorifying them, however. The novel also critiques prisoners for their failure to realize that, to change the system, they need to be committed to the common cause instead of focusing on immediate individual gain. Although *House of Slammers* justifies African American prisoners' perception that the system of imprisonment is white as a consequence of ideologies based on socio-historical realities, it also claims that without interracial collaboration individual actions, in the end, support the efforts of the prison authorities rather than subvert them.[15] Thus, by pointing out that the lack of solidarity between prisoners thwarts attempts to improve the system and reinforces institutional control, *House of Slammers* argues that racialized prison gangs, even when they are seemingly powerful, are less effective in implementing change than interracial organization.

Dannie Martin's *In the Hat* (1997) also downplays the role of gangs as a basis for racial hierarchies in prison. Set in Soledad maximum security prison, the novel recognizes the existence of prison gangs—the major local gangs consist of the members of the LA-based Monster Crips and the San Francisco-originated Dirty White Boys—as well as the potential racial conflicts instigated by them (41). Even so, the leader of the Crips, Big Mac, and Weldon Coy, a white veteran convict, take pride in the fact that they are able to "work the corners" to solve the problems between gang members nonviolently (42). Like Beans Butler in *House of Slammers,* Big Mac works as an intermediary between the various gang factions. The series of killings upon which the narrative focuses are set in motion by the murder of Weldon Coy's brother, Vern, who has "snitched" about a drug related crime outside the prison (66). Weldon and his friend Yay-Yay, a Mexican American convict, avenge the killing by eliminating the two "shot callers" of the Dirty White Boys in the prison (36, 40). The revenge killings inside create a situation that is characterized as a "prison war" (235–236).

The concept of a prison war, however, does not refer to a racial conflict between prison gangs, but rather to the manipulative measures that the prison authorities take to resolve the crisis. The correctional officer representing the prison administration testifies that the killings were committed by two black inmates even though he knows that the real murderers were the white Weldon Coy and the Mexican American Yay-Yay (237). His testimony implying that the killing is related to a "war" between competing racial prison gangs creates a conspiratorial bond between the prisoners guilty of murder and correctional officers who can then use this knowledge relationship to control the prisoners' future actions (237).

The violent events depicted in *In the Hat* suggest that gang connections between the inside and outside contribute to what takes place in the prison, but simultaneously the novel proposes that the social hierarchies inside the prison are not based on gang affiliation. That racialized identities, however, are relevant in the manipulation of these hierarchies becomes evident through the manner of which the two unidentified black characters are criminalized to produce a collaborative bond between the guilty prisoners and the correctional officers.

Some well-known prison narratives—for example, James Edward Olmos' *American Me* (1992) and Taylor Hackford's *Blood In, Blood Out* (1993)—tend to mythologize the power of prison gangs as offshoots of urban street gangs. In *American Me*, the gang leader, Santana, controls gang operations that include dealing drugs, gambling, prostitution, and extortion from the inside of Folsom prison. In *Blood In, Blood Out*, Montana, the leader of La Onda, controls drug traffic both inside and outside the prison in Los Angeles and claims that anybody who can control drug supply in prison can control the prison. These films criticize gangs by focusing on the effects of drugs on the Latino community, especially on its children, and by pointing out how the representation of Latinos as perpetrators of gang related drug crimes promotes the popular image of Latinos as criminals. *Blood In, Blood Out* also critiques prisons as racially organized institutions by representing the system as "white" and the prisoners as Latino or African American gang members who eliminate each other in gang related disputes—and, by so doing, perform their institutionally preconceived roles as "minorities" and "criminals." However, the socially critical aspects of these films are to some extent compromised by their display of the seemingly unlimited power of gangs, which suggests that resisting empowerment by gang affiliation is futile.

In *Gringo Justice* (1987), Alfredo Mirandé expresses his concern that associating Chicano prison gangs too closely with the Chicano community reinforces the view that "Mexican/Chicano culture is somehow deviant or pathological" (210). Mirandé especially blames the mass media for mobilizing bias against Chicanos, a bias that he identifies as culture specific (210). Linking the criminal activity of prison gangs with an outside ethnic or racial community does not occur in the context of whites: no attempt has been made to link the Aryan Brotherhood, for example, with Anglo communities or youth gangs outside prisons (210).

Mirandé also points out that, historically, as long as prison gang activity was seen to be part of prison culture only, gangs were not perceived as problematic, but as soon as gang activity was seen to infiltrate the society at large, gangs became a matter of public concern (209). Mirandé is highly critical of the new public perception of prison gangs as a communal problem and the credibility of the sources that generate it. He states that public knowledge of prison gangs and their spread to the community is almost exclusively based on information from "statements of law enforcement agents or their informants" (209). This information is, then, represented in a sensationalized manner by the media, which depicts it as information that is unbiased and accurate (209). Mirandé sees these media representations of prison gangs and their outside connections as problematic, especially from the perspective of the Chicano community (209).

Current anti-crime programs focusing on gang affiliation also tend to create discourse that normalizes and reinforces public perceptions that racially organized gangs are primary sources of criminal activity. The discourse created by these programs gives rise to practices aimed at apprehending the "criminals" that gang membership allegedly produced. Thus, as Christian Parenti points out in *Lockdown America: Police and Prisons in the Age of Crisis* (1999), these proactive methods do not merely "discover" delinquency, but actually *produce* criminal identities (121).[16] Parenti cites an intelligence gathering program implemented by a special police force in Fresno, California that gathers information on gang membership in "Fresno's Latino, Black, and Laotian neighborhoods" (121). Besides criminalizing gang membership as such, by targeting certain neighborhoods, the program also racializes the criminal identities it produces. The information gathered can be used to manipulate crime statistics to show higher crime solving rates than prior to the implementation of anti-gang legislation. Since the "California Street Terrorism Enforcement and Prevention Act" of 1988 criminalizes gang membership, a person who is known to be a member of a gang can be found guilty of crimes committed by other members of that gang (121). Thus, "gang crimes" can be "punished" without prosecuting the actual perpetrators.

Parenti also discusses how correctional officers use their knowledge of gang membership to incite violence in prisons. By deliberately placing rival gang members in situations in which violent one-on-one clashes are apt to erupt, prison officials stage "gladiator fights" and even videotape them for later viewing (171–172). It seems, then, that the real life manipulation of interracial relationships to produce racial conflicts is more extreme than the more covert maneuvers imagined by fiction writers. According to the institutional discourse, placing rival gang members within reach of each other functions to test the tolerance of prisoners and their "ability to get along in a controlled setting" (172). The rising number of gang related conflicts resulting from these manipulated situations provides more evidence for creating more programs to control gang activity and for more funding for special units to apprehend and incarcerate gang members

(172–173). The intelligence on gang membership is thus used to generate violence that justifies the organization of institutional hierarchies along racial lines.

Correctional officers also form their own gangs to control the power structures both between the officers themselves and between officers and prisoners, which further intensifies racialized hierarchies and gang related violence in prisons (Parenti 206–207). Racial segregation within prison staff has even led to segregated institutions: for example, "Wasco, Tehachapi, and High Desert are predominantly staffed by whites, while Lancaster is largely Black" (206). Correctional officers' gangs are clearly racially defined: officers openly proud of their KKK memberships and call themselves the SPONGE—an acronym for "Society for the Prevention of Niggers Getting Everything" (206). The primarily white and male prison staff organization into gangs seems to be a direct reaction to the increasing numbers of non-white prisoners and their presumed increased control of prison social hierarchies, a control perceived to be capable of curtailing the power of the staff. In response to the correctional officers' concerns about their diminishing authority—and in a manner contradictory to the racial segregation of prisoners—certain types of racially organized prison gangs are being broken up because they are perceived to be threats to prison officials and to the system of imprisonment itself. While racial segregation can be used to control and manipulate the social hierarchies in prison, it is also prohibited when organized racial groups seem to have become too influential.

Black Muslims were instrumental in initiating the reform of U.S. prisons in the 1960s and the 1970s. Their agenda to end legal segregation in prisons, for example, was influential not only in changing prison policies, but also contributed to the desegregation efforts in the United States in general.[17] Black Muslims were perceived to be a threat, first, because as a well organized group they appeared capable of exerting power that would "reverse patterns of race domination in the inmate subculture" (Cummins 71). Second, they were thought to be a threat because they wanted recognition as a group with "its own authority structure and communal interests"; and, third, they were seen as a threat because they initiated a significant number of court cases that "resulted in federal court intervention in prison administration" (Jacobs 66).

As African American prisoners were perceived to be gaining more power merely because of their growing proportional presence in prisons, the organization of Black Muslims was seen to be a significant threat to the non-black prison population in general and to the primarily white staff that seemed to be losing its authority in particular. To curb the growing influence of Black Muslims, prison authorities isolated Muslim leaders and forced breakups of their meetings (Cummins 71). According to one lawsuit, Muslims were not permitted to purchase or read the Koran or attend religious services, although Christian prisoners were encouraged to study the Bible and attend regular services (Hallinan 27). An organized group of prisoners, however, was not as easy to hold back as individual inmates with personal grievances. One sign of the increasing influence of the organized inmate force was the huge number of court petitions filed. In San Quentin in the 1960s, for instance, so many petitions were filed that the prison administration had to assign an office and create new jobs to handle them (Cummins 80).

What Black Muslims started for the benefit of African Americans in certain California prisons had momentous effects on the conditions of prisoners in other prisons and on the conditions of members of racial minority groups in American society in general. The protests demanding educational facilities in prisons initiated by Muslims in Folsom prison, for example, were reflected in movements at other California prisons concerning other issues such as opposition to indeterminate sentencing and demands for higher pay in prison industry jobs (Cummins 79). The demands for desegregation in prisons also resonated with political movements with similar aims in the world outside of prisons.

As a highly disciplined racially organized group, Black Muslims were perceived to pose a serious threat to the system and security of the prison in a manner similar to prison gangs. During the 1960s, the institutional discourse representing Black Muslims as a "prison gang" appealed to race and to maintaining control in prisons. Joseph Hallinan writes that, by "1962, [the] stature [of Black Muslims] was such that the convention of the American Correctional Association passed a resolution denouncing them as a "race hatred group" unworthy of the recognition granted to "bona fide religious groups" (Hallinan 25).[18] This ACA resolution supported such disciplinary methods as preventing the Muslims from reading the Koran because it saw Black Muslims primarily as a racial group, and not as a religious one. The perspective of prison authorities attempting to maintain control of prisons is expressed by Warden Joe Ragen, who reacted to a lawsuit that successfully sought Muslim prisoners such privileges as practicing their religion by stating that any concession to the Black Muslims would lead to chaos since "[t]here is absolutely no question that the Black Muslims are dedicated to destroying discipline and authority in the prison system" (Hallinan 27).

While it is a fact that most prison gangs are racially or ethnically divided and that gangs do have power in the institution of the prison, it is an exaggeration to suggest that racial hatred is their only raison d'être and that they are powerful enough to take over entire prisons. Scholars such as Alfredo Mirandé and Eric Cummins claim, for instance, that activity transcending racial lines and gang affiliations does take place in prisons. Mirandé critiques Theodore Davidson's influential study conducted in San Quentin, *Chicano Prisoners,* maintaining that it misrepresents the Chicano prisoner identity and "may promote racism and intensify racial conflict between blacks and Chicanos" (202). Mirandé's major race and gang related complaints are, first, that the study finds Chicano cultural values to be consonant with the convict code, and black values antithetical to it, and thus creates a rift between the two groups, and, second, that it does not recognize the alliances between Nuestra Familia and the Black Guerilla Family (202, 205). In his discussion of the Black Muslims, Cummins also mentions that the "Riot of '67" in San Quentin set the leaders of racial groups "to thinking of grievances that transcend race issues" (91). Therefore, to represent the riot as an aggressive conflict between the prison authority and Black Muslims who were only concerned with their particular grievances is to misrepresent it.

The current cultural fantasy holds that all modern prisons are run by gangs. There are no accurate records of how many prison gangs exist today or how many gang members there are in U.S. prisons, and since gang activity has been criminalized—in California "defined as three of more people involved in criminal activity" (Parenti 121)—it is likely that statistics will be based on estimates by the police and corrections officials only. Estimates of gang memberships in prisons range between 4 and 6 percent of the total inmate population in the United States, although some sources claim that in certain prisons gang membership is considerably higher (Hallinan 93). A state funded study of Illinois prisons found, for example, that overall 54 percent of Illinois inmates are members of a prison gang, and that in some specific prisons the number is as high as 90 percent (Hallinan 95).

In recent coverage of a "prison riot" in Oregon's Pelican Bay maximum security prison, ABC News interestingly links two incidents that it acknowledges are "unrelated" ("Thirteen" 2). In the piece covering the riot, ABC News states that two former guards were charged with "violating the civil rights of Pelican Bay inmates" by "conspiring to arrange assaults on prisoners, one of them fatal, over a nearly three-year period" (2). The main of focus of the story, however, is on the riot, and ABC News—quoting a prison spokesman—reports that "[t]he main groups of people involved were black and Hispanic. A lot of them are in street gangs, but this was more of a racial issue than a gang issue. We've had racial incidents in the past" (1). By referring to the rioters as "black and Hispanic" and as members of street gangs, the report seems both to conflate gangs and race——and to simultaneously negate the reference to gangs because this "was more of a racial issue." The spokesperson does not comment further on the assaults of individual prisoners arranged by guards.

Other prison administrators go even further in negating the existence of gangs because recognition alone would be to "legitimize" them (Hallinan 93). In the official discourse of Pennsylvania's State Correctional Institution at Graterford, for instance, gangs are referred to as "security threat groups" (Hallinan 93). These kinds of practices that manipulate correctional discourse on prison gangs, either by mixing the concepts of race and gangs or by denying the existence of gangs altogether, obscure the issue itself and its representation in public discourse.[19]

Effacing the presence of prison gangs by denying their existence or by renaming them seems indicative of a larger "disappearing" project taking place in the U.S. discourse on criminality. As Angela Davis writes, the problem of poverty in the United States is being veiled in the discourse of criminality, and incarceration seems to be performing the magic trick of making "[h]omelessness, unemployment, drug addiction, mental illness, and illiteracy" disappear "in order to convey the illusion of solving social problems" ("Masked" 1). Davis also notes that "colored bodies" constitute the main raw material in creating this illusion, since the U.S. "political economy of prisons relies on racialized assumptions of criminality" (3).

In a manner similar to the way that the political economy of the prison relies on racialized assumptions of who the criminals are, the prison's discursive practices manipulate the public understanding of the social hierarchies of incarcerated people by racializing their identities and, by so doing, misrepresenting them. The meaning of race as a governing notion in the discourse of prison policies is not a reference to individual prisoner identities, but to a tool of prison management, and as such reflects social and historical ideologies that inform racial hierarchies in the United States.[20] Thus, by basing their discursive hierarchies on race, prison practices continue the tradition of social and political racial containment that privileges whites as non-racial.

The contemporary prison novel counteracts this tendency to obscure the meaning of race by proposing other non-racial models of social hierarchies in prison. The tradition of the prison novel is not postracial,[21] since its characterization is structured racially, but its racialization functions to comment on the institutional and political discourses on criminality. The contemporary prison novel demonstrates that prisoner characters are not conditioned to follow the racial-hierarchical configurations of institutional discourse, and, by uncovering these ideological configurations, suggests alternative ways of representing imprisoned individuals and their interaction. By refusing to play their predetermined roles in the racialized hierarchies of the prison, characters in the prison novel reveal that these hierarchies, in fact, originate with the institution, and are not spontaneously or politically formed by the inmates.

Chapter Four

Surveillance and Prisoner Identity: Imprisoned Bodies as the American Other

When the Italian clothes manufacturer Benetton launched a 2000 advertising campaign featuring U.S. death row inmates, it evoked a major public outrage.[1] Part of the "We, On Death Row" campaign was comprised of a series of interviews with death row inmates and their images appearing in a 96 page supplement to *Talk* magazine. The inmates posing in their prison garb—mostly in close-ups—stare directly at the camera. Some segments of their interviews appear as double-paged aphoristic statements, such as the murderer John Lotter's comment, "I think people like seeing other people suffer and killed."[2] Although the campaign was simultaneously launched in 60 countries, its focus on death row inmates is particularly resonant in the United States because the United States is the only Western country still using the death penalty.[3]

The campaign that Benetton characterized as "look[ing] reality in the face"—and its critics characterized as immoral and banal "shockvertising"—was primarily criticized for victimizing various groups of people (Benetton 2; Garfield 45). The alleged victims of the campaign were, first of all, the unsuspecting consumers caught off guard by the campaign. *Advertising Age* magazine's Bob Garfield writes that the campaign was "a cowardly assault on the sensibilities of unsuspecting readers, who have no expectation to be confronted with human tragedy by the ready-to-wear industry" (45). Other alleged victims were the retail giant SEARS, which canceled its exclusive contract with Benetton, the Missouri penitentiary where the interviews and photo-ops took place, the "exploited" inmates themselves, and the victims of the crimes that these inmates committed

(Simon A5). The harsh comments of advertising guru Bob Garfield even suggest that the whole advertising business was still another major victim of Benetton's aim of "giving back a human face to the prisoners on death row" (Benetton 1).

It was clear that, by replacing images of the "beautiful people" with those of criminals, Benetton infringed upon the rules of the iconography of advertising, and thus created dissonance between the expectations of commercial cultural representation and its consumers. To use Michel de Certeau's terminology related to cultural "poaching," Benetton seems to see itself as a "tactician" who manipulates a moment of social and historical specificity in the United States, while the advertisement industry sees Benetton as an institution which, by transgressing the rules of advertising, also violates the code of corporate behavior (Ek 8–10).

In addition to violating the tradition of corporate behavior and misusing the discursive realm of advertising, Benetton also violated the sense of how American consumers expect to see prisoners represented in mass culture. Prisoners are not expected to invade the cultural space reserved for heroes and celebrities, or to challenge consumers by returning their scrutinizing gaze—as if the prisoners actually were part of *us,* as the capital "We" in the campaign title implies. According to the public perception, the image of the male imprisoned body should not undermine the position or question the authority of the ones who look *at* it.

Instead, the public wants, and expects, prisoners as objects of the cultural and national gaze to be surveyed in prisons, through bars and peepholes and on the monitors of surveillance cameras. These institutionalized images are then repeated in the visual media, which in a way doubles the act of surveillance. The act of surveillance in the context of prison narratives means both the end of privacy and an opening for private, fetishized peeping. While prisoners as the isolated objects of surveillance lose their privacy, the consumers of the images produced by the visual media gain an opportunity to watch without being seen. At the same time, the possibility of an open, public gaze—and the gaze back, as suggested by the Benetton campaign—is obliterated.

This chapter analyzes how constant surveillance, or being continuously looked at, defines the production of prisoner identity. I focus on the prisoner as the "national other" by expanding on the facets of otherness discussed in previous chapters—criminal, racial, and sexual otherness—and by adding the dimension of visuality. I consider how the criminalizing, racist, and homophobic institutional and public gaze[4] informs prisoner subjectivity in a panoptic manner. In other words, my primary focus is not on surveillance as such, but on how surveillance constructs a prisoner subjectivity that both reproduces and resists the cultural fantasy of what prisoners are like. I am particularly interested in self-identification in autobiographical prison narratives, specifically in Sanyika Shakur's *Monster: The Autobiography of an L.A. Gang Member* (1993) and Eldridge Cleaver's *Soul on Ice* (1968).

First, I argue that prison narratives produce a prisoner subjectivity that, in part, emulates the identity that preexists in the images produced by the visual media. The representations of prisoner identity in prison films and TV shows are reproduced by other prison narratives—such as autobiographical texts—through the focus on the prisoner body, for example. The male body is turned into a *prisoner* body by prosthetic means such as bodybuilding and tattoos that both identify it as an imprisoned body and at the same time resist institutional markings such as mandatory prison uniforms aimed at unifying prisoners' bodies. In this context, I also discuss how the visual media often specularizes and fetishizes African American and Latino male bodies and, thus, reinforces stereotypic conceptions of black and Latino masculinity as corporeal.

Second, I argue that prison narratives primarily use the mirror as a trope for seeing the other rather than the self for the purposes of security, communication, and information. Metaphorically, then, the mirror also constructs the self as "other," as a panoptic reflection of the prisoner identity that is being looked at. Since the self is constructed through seeing the other, the narcissistic aspect of seeing oneself is also indirect, as is exemplified in Cleaver's *Soul on Ice* in the narrator's desire to see himself through the eyes of somebody else.

Third, I argue that "the look"—a steady challenging gaze—is used as a disciplinary measure to produce types of prisoner masculinity that contest the identity that it aims to construct. "The look" is used, for example, as a way to highlight the hierarchical differences between the prison staff and prisoners, or between prisoners. It is also used as an emasculating strategy that feminizes prisoner subjectivity by making prisoners the objects of a controlling gaze, or by indicating femininity in male-male relationships. The immediacy of "the look" makes the work done by surveillance technologies more personal and reinforces the effect of being constantly watched.

In *Discipline and Punish: The Birth of the Prison* (1975), Michel Foucault claims that "[o]ur society is one not of spectacle, but of surveillance . . . We are . . . in the panoptic machine, invested by its effects of power, which we bring to ourselves since we are part of its mechanism" (217).

Foucault's theory of modern Western society refers to the Panopticon, the 18th century utilitarian philosopher Jeremy Bentham's plan for the ideal prison. Bentham's plan has become one of the central cultural icons of our time, primarily through Foucault's work in the 1970s. The Panopticon, a prison in which prisoners can be surveyed without the prisoners seeing the surveyor, ideally produces the outcome that prisoners, internalizing the idea of constant surveillance, begin to monitor their own behavior even when the actual external surveillance does not exist.

Some social scientists and cultural critics have also characterized the modern-day United States as a surveillance society, a society in which the boundaries between the private and the public have become blurred.[5] Without fully realizing the extent of it, human beings have become objects of physical, visual, and electronic surveillance in their everyday lives. Medical institutions keep records of patients' mental and bodily conditions, bank customers are visually surveyed by cameras at ATM machines, and grocery-store membership cards register and track consumer shopping behavior.[6] People may consent to these kinds of surveillance because they view them to be beneficial and consider being excluded from these practices worse than being included in them (Whitaker 139–140).

Reg Whitaker terms these types of social and commercial surveillance "consensual," or "participatory Panopticon" (139). Although Whitaker metaphorizes the United States as a surveillance society involving citizens as objects who participate in and consent to surveillance in a panoptic manner, he also points out a crucial dissimilarity between Foucault's notion and his own application of it. In the context of the Panopticon, the omniscient surveillance is imaginary, but in our society it is *real*—and takes the form of multiple technologies that keep track of our lives (140). Therefore, to some extent our consenting to this surveillance is illusory because we do not seem to have any other choice but to consent.

Stephen Paul Miller also points to the Panopticon-like effects of surveillance, but instead of focusing on the societal or commercial surveillance of citizens, he describes U.S. culture itself *as* surveillance. Using this concept of culture as surveillance, Miller discusses, for example, how identities are produced through cultural "self-surveillance" (2). He writes, "I define surveillance broadly as the monitoring and regimenting of an object, an institution, an area, a group, or a person, and *self-surveillance* as a self-monitoring and a self-regimenting that sometimes *reinforces identifications* put into place by external surveillance" (2, my italics). As one example of cultural "self-surveillance" reinforcing identifications, Miller notes the impact of the feminist movement: "In the seventies, for instance, a woman could take on the identity of a feminist, and her consciousness could be raised by a heightened awareness of that identity" (19).

Miller considers the opportunity to use "identity prisms" such as the feminist identity as "invaluable to personal and social development" because they "indicate the power of the individual to try on and 'buy into' identity" (19). As a counterpoint to the empowering effects of cultural surveillance, Miller discusses the post-World War II intensification of the "myth of American identity" illustrated by the surveillance work done by the House Committee on Un-American Activities, for example (187–188). The process of eliminating what is *not* part of American identity required an "other" as the object of surveillance through which to foreground and marginalize various minority positions (187–188). In addition to political minorities, racial minorities remained outside of that which is American, as is evident in the insistence of identifying such national authors as James Baldwin as "Negro" writers rather than American writers (187–188).

Prison narratives provide an epitomic discursive site for the analysis of the dual effects of social and cultural surveillance that Miller describes: the empowerment gained through self-surveillance, and the "othering" performed by external surveillance in order to marginalize or exclude minority positions. Now that the U.S. prison system has abandoned the ideals of reform and penitence, the main function of the prison is to keep inmates locked up and under surveillance. As a method of external surveillance that transforms its objects into the other, prisons seem to both invite and legitimize the sadistic, masochistic, and voyeuristic fantasy and pleasure of looking at life in prison. The punishment and surveillance functions of correctional institutions authorize the access of the public gaze to the private body of the prisoner, and thus also legalize the dynamics of fantasy and pleasure that the body under display and discipline produces. Constructing the prisoner as the object of the public gaze also affirms the hierarchies of difference between the social and moral standards of the ones who look and the ones being looked at.

Yet, in a society characterizing itself as a surveillance society and which, as a result of excessive surveillance, feels like a society of prisoners, it is evidently difficult to establish a clear difference between the subjects and objects of surveillance. As William Staples points out, there are too many "Tiny Brothers" doing the "Big Brother" job for us to be able to say who the surveyors and the surveyed are (2). People who use email and everyday household devices such as CallerIDs subject themselves to being surveyed by an indefinite number of other people, and by doing so, become, even if not consciously participants at least collaborators in a "culture of voyeurs." This culture of voyeurs also encourages people to enjoy visual representations of themselves and others on television shows like *America's Funniest Videos* and on websites reporting on people's lives in real time (Staples 57).

In order to fully establish the difference between the real prisoners and members of the rest of society—that is, to conceptualize the otherness of the criminal—the discourses of the visual media provide viewers an image of the prisoner that confirms the cultural fantasy of a prisoner identity. First of all, the visual media tends to spectacularize crime and criminals. In the guise of documentaries, for example, viewers are offered dramatized representations of crime: as Palmer has noted, our "gaze is narrowed as we stare at spectacles of crime that confirm the prejudices learnt elsewhere in television's spectrum" (Palmer 101). These spectacles of crime reinforce the difference between the spectator and the other through focusing on the social, moral, and sexual deviance of prisoners, which is metaphorized and fetishized through narrative attention to dirt, bodily functions, violence, and sexual perversion.

On televised crime shows, the image of the criminal is usually represented by blurry or digitalized pictures, or by mug shots showing angry, distorted, unshaven faces. In *Seven Long Times*, Piri Thomas claims that the media coerces suspected or convicted criminals to act in ways that make their images look criminal and dangerous. He narrates an incident in which a representative of a crime magazine kept taunting him with racial slurs until, Thomas says, he "turned and felt [his] face twist into a snarl. [His] mouth opened and hurled a torrent of curses" (30–31). Thus, the reporter got the kind of image of a criminal—of the "goddam dirty nigger"—that he wanted (30).

Discourses that spectacularize criminality also give people visible evidence that the criminal justice system works, that dangerous criminals have been incarcerated, and that this has happened, in part, as a result of the actions of audiences of shows like *America's Most Wanted*.[7] As the final stage in establishing the difference between the criminal and the non-criminal, the imprisoned, textualized bodies of prisoners are used to visualize incarceration as an effective form of punishment. Spectacularizing narratives focus on the vulnerability of bodies in shower rooms, on the necessity of shackling prisoners and treating them in a rough manner, and on corporeal suffering—including rape—as part of punishment. As one inmate puts it, the popular perception is that, "[i]f the prisoner is not in obvious pain and anguish, if he is not being made to visibly suffer, punishment is not being properly administered" (Carlson 44).

Since the sadistic pleasure people get from observing the visualized pain and suffering of prisoners in the media is sanctioned by the criminal justice system, the concerns about the loss of human dignity expressed by surveillance theorists are not applied to these representations of prisoner subjectivity. When theorists discuss the problems of our modern-day "surveillance society," they see the loss of personhood and human dignity as one of the major dangers of being surveyed in the ways in which people are now surveyed; in the case of visualized, textualized representations of prisoner identity, however, the loss of personhood seems to be understood as part of the punishment that prisoners duly deserve.[8] Instead of being a morally or ethically questionable activity, then, watching the prisoner as the national other is beneficial because it bolsters the contemporary American identity of good, law abiding citizens who are ready to respond to the call for toughness on crime.

Constant visual surveillance is not problematic from the point of view of the institution of the prison either. Prisons use visual surveillance to "monitor the movement of prisoners, to protect guards, to protect prisoners from one another, and to protect prisoners from undue use of force or abuse by prison guards, especially in women's prisons" (Petersen 8–3). Officially, surveillance cameras in prisons function as a protective measure that either monitors or prevents unwanted human contact. However, they also prevent sexual contacts between consenting adults (like other "protective" measures such as the separation of homosexual inmates from each other) and provide material for viewing staff-organized "gladiator" fights between inmates.

In *Discipline and Punish*, Foucault writes that the "major effect of the Panopticon [is] to induce in the inmate a state of conscious and permanent visibility that assures the automatic functioning of power"(201). Prison narratives form a panoptic system that makes visible a prisoner identity that functions as an object of social and cultural surveillance in which all participate. As a form of *external surveillance,* to use the terminology of Stephen Paul Miller, prison narratives, by spectacularizing criminal identity, transform the prisoner into the national other and, therefore, hold the kind of representational power that is central to the panoptic machinery. In this sense, for the inmate, the image of himself on television reminds him not only of "the freedom he has lost," but also of the public perception of his prisoner identity, (Carlson 44). Thus the "privilege" of having access to television in prison works as a subtle form of punishment—as a way of exercising representational power over prisoner subjectivity, and as a reinforcement of that subjectivity as the other.

From the perspective of empowering *self-surveillance,* however, prison narratives do not merely reproduce the public image of the prisoner identity, but refuse to accept it, and thus invert the othering process by relocating representational power in the prisoner. Thus, prisoner subjectivity is produced by the various modes of textualized external surveillance and self-surveillance is produced by discourses representing criminology, sociology, psychology, and literary and popular culture. These discourses collapse the representational spheres of the public and the private by reproducing the public image in the private identity and, simultaneously, fuse the subject and object of surveillance by emulating the object of external surveillance in a panoptic manner.

The complexity of the panoptic process can be recognized in the manner in which both the seemingly transparent prisoner identities and their revised formulations appear in the same or similar cultural productions. As discussed in earlier chapters, prison narratives resist and revise the popular prisoner identity within the contexts of racialized, sexualized, and moral criminality. Racially motivated self-definitions focus on empowerment through education, autobiographical texts use narrative distancing of the self from the scenes of violent rapes, and filmic narratives focus on the heroic escapes of the wrongfully incarcerated.

In *Monster: The Autobiography of an L.A. Gang Member* (1993), Sanyika Shakur traces his development from a member of the L.A.-based Crips gang into a prisoner and a spokesperson for the nationalist New Afrikan prison movement.[9] At the time of the publication of his book, Shakur was twenty-nine years old and serving time in the Pelican Bay Special Housing Unit (xiii; "Sanyika" 1). His most notable literary and ideological influences are Malcolm X and the New Afrikan Nation movement: he models his autobiography after the *Autobiography of Malcolm X* and shapes his discussion of his growth into racial, social, and religious awareness after the ideology of the New Afrikan Nation.

Shakur seems to aim at writing a narrative of empowering *self-surveillance,* but because his autobiography focuses on the body, sex, and physical violence, it fails to do so and instead reinscribes the stereotype of black male identity as primarily corporeal, and thus reproduces popular representations of African American criminal otherness. Another reason that *Monster* does not evolve into a narrative of empowerment is Shakur's lack of significant personal growth. That, at the end of his narrative, Shakur is still in prison—this time serving 17 years for assault and grand theft auto—demonstrates that he has not managed to, in the tradition of African American autobiographers such Malcolm X, "turn his life around" (379).

Shakur begins his autobiography from a world-scale perspective by referring to the gang wars in Los Angeles as a "civil war" that lasted nine years longer than the war in Vietnam and went on unnoticed by the United Nations (xi-xii). He announces the empowering aim of his autobiography by stating that he wrote *Monster* "out of desperation for the survival of the youths and civilians who are directly and indirectly involved in the fighting" in order to "help work out workable solutions for all concerned" (xiv). However, the only solution he offers—without arguing for it explicitly—is separatism (382). He also ends his narrative in a defeatist mode with, "We cannot contaminate [our children] with our feuds of madness, which are predicated on factors over which we have no control," as the last sentence of his book (383).

Monster retains the image of black masculinity as violent, sexual, and corporeal. Although the focus on the body is particularly strong when Shakur narrates his evolution from a "gangbanger" into a prisoner through his bodily transformation, his body and his outward appearance are foregrounded from the very beginning of the text. Shakur dedicates his autobiography to his mother, Birdie M. Scott, who "had the courage to push [him] out in a world of which [they] control so little" (v). The dedication speaks of Shakur's awakening to the ideological goals of his literary work and his existence—the aim of gaining more control of the world in which he lives—but also focuses on the corporeal aspect of his birth. Likewise, the first incident that he narrates in the actual text of his autobiography draws attention to a bodily gesture: Shakur is being punished for flashing the Crips sign in a class photograph (3–4). His initiation into the Crips gang also involves violently physical tests, including being beaten up and kicked by his fellow gang members (9).

Shakur carefully narrates the various clothes and prison uniforms that define moments of his personal evolution. He points out, for example, how the Los Angeles County Jail separates incarcerated 150 Crips members from the general population of 18,000 inmates by placing them into a segregated unit and by outfitting them with a different uniform than the rest of the inmates. Wearing gray jumpsuits instead of the usual blue ones, the gang members, who are primarily black, appeared to have been marked as targets; they "stood out like flies in the buttermilk" (279). In addition to marking his prisoner body, clothing also defines his newfound religion. Shakur describes his embarrassment when he first enters the Islamic Center in Los Angeles. While the rest of the congregation wears elaborate "Afrikan" dress, he, in his "501s, Puma tennis shoes, a Polo shirt, and a Raiders cap" feels like "a damn fool!" (255). Shakur also takes pride in being a pioneer in introducing certain types of fashions, although his "dress code often brought down the wrath of the deputies" (373). He wore "a red, black, and green fez, a black t-shirt, and black fatigues bloused over [his] combat boots . . . long before hip-hop made it fashionable" (373).

It is ironic that the prison garb originally designed to humiliate the prisoner is now a fashionable outfit, made popular by rap artists who are often ex-inmates themselves. The rap artists' baggy pants originated in prison as an assertion of masculinity: "anyone wearing pants too tight would be considered effeminate" (Farr 2). Prison uniforms also had the practical purpose of helping law enforcement catch escaped prisoners—as we have learned from prison films, the first thing an escapee must do is find clothing to replace his striped or bright orange uniform. The popularity of prison fashion indicates how integral prisons are to U.S. culture. It has become part of popular culture because prison is a shared experience, either as a lived experience or an experience mediated by cultural products inspired by it. Making prison uniforms into sought after fashionable items also turns an act intended to humiliate prisoners into an act of empowering self-definition, an act signifying control rather than submission.

The influence of popular culture is often referred to in prison autobiographies and usually these references are ironic, as is Piri Thomas' comment on his initiation into the prison workout routine in his *Seven Long Times* (1974). Thomas notes that "[m]ovies can give you some idea" when he grasps the bars of his cell and does some "light pushaways" (54). Thus, he is conscious of his performance of the prisoner identity naturalized by the bodybuilder image of the prisoner represented in cinema.

Shakur, on the other hand, takes his bodybuilding exercises in prison quite seriously. Through narrative focus on his body, Shakur represents the development of his prisoner identity, including his racialized prison sexuality and the change in his ideological stance on race. At the same time that his body grows, so grows his reputation among inmates. After heavily investing in bodybuilding, Shakur is "physically the second biggest in the institution"—he has twenty and one-quarter inch biceps and bench presses four hundred and seventy pounds—and simultaneously his "reputation balloons": his "rep" is "omnipresent, totally saturating every circle of gang life . . . Monster Kody had arrived" (208). He also "quickly made the transition from soldier to sergeant of arms to intelligence officer" in the Afrikan Nation faction of the prisoners (348). He gets the model for his "Mafia-style gangsterism" in prison from Mario Puzo's *The Godfather,* which for him represents the Italians' sense of who they are, of their understanding of their cultural heritage (207–208).

Shakur also narrates his growing awareness of what being African American—or "New Afrikan," in his nationalist terminology—means to him through focusing on the body, and on skin color in particular. He describes, for example, his mentor in prison, Muhammad Abdullah, as "about six feet even, with a very dark, shiny, well-kept blackness," and his fellow Crip, Tookie, as a huge man with "twenty-two inch arms [and a] fifty-eight-inch chest," and as "dark, Marcus Garvey dark, shiny, slick, and strong" (213, 247). Thus, for Shakur, the nationalist ideology of racial separatism manifests itself in the size and the darkness of the imprisoned black male body.

Another manifestation of the ideological underpinnings that inform prisoner identity and New Afrikan nationalist thought in Shakur's text is his frequent use of the metaphor of war. The militancy of his representation of life in prison is, first of all, apparent in his diction: guards are "soldier-cops" and inmates of the New Afrikan Nation are "soldiers" with officers of various ranks. Thus, the relationship between the New Afrikan inmates and the correctional officers is depicted as one of open war, with the military organization of the New Afrikan Nation proactively aiming at controlling the prison. The war is not limited to inside the prison walls, however. Once Shakur has acquired an awareness of his racial heritage—he knows he comes from Afrika—he considers himself "a soldier of [his] people, all citizens of the C[rip]-Nation" (338). Therefore, his perception of society at large is that of an ongoing war between various groups of people, primarily identified as racialized gangs such as the Crips, Bloods, and the Mexican Mafia, and as "civilians"—particularly wives and children—who fall victim to the war and are in need of protection (382).

The corporeal and racialized nature of Shakur's representation of the black male prison identity also figures into his remarks about gender and sexuality. He discusses attacks on the African American inmates' "private parts," both by white inmates and correctional officers as part of racist treatment in prison. He writes, for example, that "pigs" "were always antagonistically aggressive" toward black inmates and their "dicks"—that it seemed as if some "personal grudge" existed between white men and the black men's dicks (279, 139). In addition to commenting on racism in prison, then, foregrounding the black penis by equating "us" with "our dicks" reproduces the cultural perception that African American masculinity is equal to the body, and to the penis in particular.

Although Shakur's "buff" body evoked the respect of fellow inmates in prison and appreciative looks from his wife and relatives, his body image clashes with his self-identification as a spokesperson for the New Afrikan

Independence Movement. Shakur writes that, once he had decided to distance himself from the Crips gang, he gives up weightlifting and creates a new "sleek, defined, limber body" (356). Another sign of the ideological changes he has experienced is that he tells his gang-member friends not to call him "Monsta" or "nigga" any longer—he has changed his name to Sanyika (362).

In addition to bodybuilding, tattoos are commonly used to construct the prisoner body. By marking his body with tattoos, the prisoner defies the institutional marking of the body that unifies prisoners by making wearing prison uniforms mandatory, and by so doing also negates the prisoners' individuality. However, since there are dominant themes in prison tattoos throughout prisoner communities, a "prison" tattoo tends to result in another kind of uniformity instead of erasing the institutional marking of the body.[10] As part of prison fashion outside the prison, tattoo artists make tattoos look "authentically" prison-originated by using only black ink because colors are not usually available to prison artists (Farr 1). Even though many traditional tattoos, such as the "pachuco cross" and Crips and Bloods insignia are specifically gang-related rather than prison-related, tattoos strongly denote the prisoner body. Recently, social programs have been established to fund the removal of tattoos because they stigmatize young Latino and African American males in particular as criminals (Salas 300).

During his time in prison, Shakur's identity changes from a self-defined "criminal" at the age of sixteen into a "soldier" in the Afrikan Nation when he is in his mid to late twenties (138). In *Monster*, the potentially empowering notion of the possibility of personal growth in prison is marred, however, by the text's lack of significant insight into the ways in which the U.S. criminal justice system and society criminalize African American masculinity. While Shakur opposes the Rodney King kind of racist media objectification of the black man—he says it is "not so much the beating itself . . . but the repeated *sight of it*" (380, my italics) that signifies the criminalizing process for him—he simultaneously spectacularizes and fetishizes the black imprisoned male body in much the same way that the visual media does. He foregrounds his own acculturation into prisoner identity by focusing on the development of his prisoner body and defines black male prisoner subjectivity by focusing on the role of penis, skin color, and hyper-masculine militancy in a violent civil war both inside and outside the prison. Thus, Shakur reproduces the cultural image of black male criminality in a panoptic manner, by becoming part of the machinery that creates and recreates that image, and reflects his anxiety about his own masculinity through another person's appreciating gaze upon his body.

Robyn Wiegman describes the fetishization of blackness in "mass-mediated visual technologies" as a result of the late 20th century attempt of African American "representational integration" backfiring (*American* 116). She claims that the inclusion of African American characterization in both popular culture and the literary canon ignores the question of political power and simply fetishizes blackness (116). As discussed in Chapter One, this type of fetishization also takes place in prison films such as *No Escape,* in which the only major African American character is also the only major character who constantly wears a tank top that reveals his bulging muscles. As Wiegman points out, the fetishization of the African American body adds "commodity value" to blackness, a point not without irony in a country "where the literal commodification of the body under enslavement is now simulated in representational circuits" (116, 117).[11] The fetishizing of the body is even more ironic, I believe, when it is performed under the auspices of empowering the criminalized black male, and of offering solutions to end his criminalization.

Shakur does acknowledge the feasibility of his political activism and claims that the ideologues of the New Afrikan movement, himself included, made the same mistakes as Black Panthers did by "importing revolutionary ideas" such as Marxism and communism and failing to see that these ideas failed to connect with the "concrete conditions" to which they were applied, by "falling prey to parochialism and tribalism," and by not gaining "mass appeal" (349). He does not, however, ponder the political validity of his autobiographical work and the representation of black masculinity in prison that it offers. His representational vehicle follows the tradition of the Black Power Movement, and of the Black Panthers—the tradition of hyper-masculine militant ideals that tend to subdue and neglect the female gender, and that have been criticized for that since the time the ideals were first proliferated. Thus, it seems that Shakur's *Monster* repeats representational models of black manhood that not only fetishize blackness, but also have been challenged as counter-productive.

In his classic prison autobiography, *Soul on Ice* (1968), Eldridge Cleaver, another African American political activist, represents black incarcerated masculinity through the lens of watching and being looked at. Like Shakur's *Monster,* Cleaver's *Soul on Ice* makes it clear that its purpose is to define African American masculinity in a self-empowering manner. As the title implies, Cleaver's text has the soul as its starting point. Instead of privileging the implied inward look, however, Cleaver's narrative focuses on watching others as a metaphor for prison life and being looked at as a defining factor in the construction of prisoner identity. As a result, vision and visuality strongly inform his sense of his subjectivity as an African American man in prison. Since Cleaver frequently considers others' gazes as mirrors reflecting his own prisoner identity, his narrative also constructs his self as "other"—as a panoptic reflection of the identity that he sees in the eyes of others.[12]

Maxwell Geismar writes that, in Cleaver's autobiography, "the central problem is of *identification* as a black soul which has been 'colonized' . . . by an oppressive white society that projects its brief, narrow vision of life as eternal truth" (9). Referring to Du Bois' *The Souls of Black Folk,* Geismar implies that Du Bois' notion that "the 'souls of black folk' are the best mirror in which to see the white American self" also applies to Cleaver's text (10). Indeed, Cleaver discusses how white American masculinity is defined, in part, by controlling the image of black manhood. He cites Muhammad Ali's success as a heavyweight champion as a turning point in this regard. According to Cleaver, up to the point when Ali refused to be controlled by the white "puppet-master," the African American male body had been used to define white masculinity as superior to black masculinity because the public image of the black champion had been manipulated and "tamed by the white man" (92–93). As such, the visual image of the African American male as the other constructed white American masculinity.

In the tradition of African American autobiography, Cleaver's representation of his prisoner identity partially inverts this notion; black masculinity is looked at and defined in terms of its relation to white masculinity. At the beginning of *Soul on Ice,* Cleaver discusses how his self-education in prison changed his perception of white America—in prison he began to look at white America through "new eyes" (25). By asserting that he "watches America" from his prison cell, Cleaver suggests that he is turning the tables on who is watching whom, but his constant references to being the object of surveillance in prison and to his losing his identity has the effect of refuting this claim. In addition, Cleaver's sense of losing his identity in prison at least in part comes from *not* being looked at. He writes that part of being a man outside of prison is getting confirmation of one's masculinity from the "constant feedback" of women's gazes—from "the number of female heads [a man] turns" (28). The manner in which Cleaver laments the denied opportunity of seeing the reflection of his own masculinity in the eyes of women adds a narcissistic element to the construction of his prisoner identity.

Nevertheless, in prison being looked at is a source of anxiety for Cleaver. Instead of gazes that confirm his attractiveness to women, in prison he only gets "hate-stares and sour frowns" (28). Those hate-stares are so powerful that only in a cell with an "impregnable door" instead of bars can he relax and feel safe because only there, where nobody can see him, does he "not have watch the other convicts any more or the guards in the gun towers" (51). Even relaxation in prison involves watching or being watched. The "free" time is spent either watching television, or "watching the other convicts who are watching other convicts" play games, beat on the punching bag, or lift weights in the prison yard (51–52).

Imprisonment produces both the anxiety about being looked at and the desire to be looked at. The desire to be looked at arises from the need for affirmation of one's masculinity, and, in *Soul on Ice,* that need manifests itself in Cleaver's consciousness about his body and his way of narrating his body so that we must look at it in detail and in the nude. At the beginning of his autobiography, he describes his body "in prison" as a Negro body that is tall, skinny, in the need of a shave, and "hard-up enough to suck [his] grandmother's old withered tits" (30). He also wishes to be able to get "*clean*" again, both in a "steam-bath sense" and in an "*Esquire* sense" (30). Cleaver also foregrounds his naked body in his description of his daily "calisthenics" routine, by inviting his readers to imagine his body when he does his "kneebends, butterflies, touching [his] toes, squats, [and] wind-mills" (49).[13]

The desire to be looked at also signifies Cleaver's desire to be seen as an individual in an environment that aims at suppressing individuality. In a letter to his legal advisor, Beverly Axelrod, Cleaver expresses his frustration about feeling "invisible" because in prison his individual identity is not recognized (133). Part of being a prisoner is learning how *not* to look at any-body in particular, in any way in particular—in order to enhance one's own invisibility and to avoid becoming a target of challenging gazes—although "some henchmen" Cleaver mentions in this context *want* to be recognized by a glance in order to maintain their position of power and control (133).

The anxiety about being looked at—aside from the threat to personal safety engendered by hateful stares—arises from the manner in which sexuality is constructed through male-male gazes in prison. As discussed in Chapter Two in the context of Nathan McCall's *Makes Me Wanna Holler,* male gazes on male bodies feminize the object of the gaze and are believed to have the effect of "turning" that objectified prisoner into a homosexual. In prison films, this homophobic anxiety is often managed through the negation of homosexuality, either by idealizing such hyper-masculine pro-tagonists as Clint Eastwood in *Escape from Alcatraz* or by fixing the male gaze on a fetishized female figure that asserts heterosexuality such as the poster of Rita Hayworth in *Shawshank Redemption*. In *Soul on Ice*, Cleaver narrates his frustrating experience with a poster of a white "pinup girl" from *Esquire* magazine. A correctional officer rips Cleaver's poster down, telling him that he should get himself "a colored girl for a pinup— no white women" (21). Cleaver is not even allowed to look at a picture of a white woman because his gaze upon the white body challenges the white male guard's need to control both white femininity and black masculinity.[14]

Cleaver also describes other pictures on the walls of his cell, pictures that construct his prisoner identity through focusing on his ideological development and his need to express affinity with the people that the images represent. The pictures on the walls represent what is absent in prison life: pictures of women that represent heterosexual relationships and idolized figures that represent an assertion of an ideological bond. For example, Cleaver replaces the image of Elijah Muhammad in his cell with "a beautiful picture of Malcolm X" suggesting the change in his religious and racial ideology (62). When Cleaver starts looking at the picture of Malcolm X, his former Muslim friends stop looking at him, which invests in the image on the wall the power to transform relationships between inmates (62).

Various ways of watching and being watched construct Cleaver's sense of his prisoner masculinity. He longs, in a narcissistic manner, to be looked at by women whose gazes would reaffirm his crumbling sense of his manhood; he wants to see his own masculinity reflected in the admiring eyes of the women. It seems that his desire to be looked at as a man and as an individual expresses a lack of empowerment in his prisoner subjectivity rather than the achievement of empowerment that is the goal of his writing. In a complex way, then, visual exchanges in prison are primarily a source of anxiety because they seemingly have the power to change the prisoners' sexual orientation from heterosexual to homosexual, for instance, and their absence may mark you as an inmate disrespectful of prisoner hierarchies and, therefore, deserving of punishment.

Looks between prisoners and between prisoners and correctional officers can function as emotional and psychological ways to injure and to punish (Carlson 46). The immediacy of the "look" used as a means of punishment intensifies and individualizes the work done by institutional external surveillance by various technical means. Wayne Carlson, a long term offender, writes in the Canadian *Journal of Prisoners on Prisons* that "the advocates of the "lock'em up throw away the key" philosophy have no real idea of what prison does to the hearts, minds, and souls of the prisoners"— they believe that the "physical, emotional and psychological pain that one can see with the naked eye is the only real form of punishment" (43–44). Since physical punishment in prisons is currently outlawed, it has been replaced by "emotional and psychological ways to injure," by "looks, body language, and tone of voice" (46). Carlson also writes, quoting another inmate, that having the privileges of television and radio in your cell and private visits by family members is like "being buried up to the neck in the middle of the street; we can see life flow around us but we can't get up to take part in it" (45). Even the commodities and circumstances that appear to the public to be undeserved privileges work in subtle ways to punish inmates by letting them repeatedly see what they want but cannot have.

Since daily life in prison "remains as mysterious as the dark side of the moon," publications like *Journal of Prisoners on Prisons* and the *Stop Prisoner Rape* website aim at raising public awareness of crime and criminality from the prisoner's point of view (Carlson 43). These publications also counteract television shows like Ted Koppel's "Crime and Punishment" and *America's Most Wanted,* the apparent function of which is to guarantee viewer satisfaction by offering them masochistic and sadistic pleasure as well as "proof" that the prison as a system that punishes actually works. In fact, *America's Most Wanted* recently reincarnated itself by adding the subtitle, "America Fights Back," which gives the show a new urgency and its viewers a sense of control in the fight against wanted criminals in America. In a manner similar to Foucault's paradigm shift from the focus on the late 19th century European acts of medicalized "perversions" to the persons who perform the acts, the 20th century U.S. social and cultural perception has refocused the idea of criminality from the acts of crime to the criminals who perform those acts.

In particular, the surveillance performed by the visual media constructs the prisoner as the personification of criminality and, thus, as the racial, sexual, and criminal other of America. The consumers of cultural products need and use the prisoner as the national other in order to construct their own social and cultural selves as superior, and to be able to punish and laugh at themselves through the image of the prisoner. Thus, consumers turn the representations of prisoner perversions into their own perverted pleasure. Only in *prison-related* films and TV shows can male-male gang rapes be funny, for example.[15] Outside of the narrative, as outside observers looking at the other, viewers can gain pleasure from acts that defy fundamental notions of human dignity. Prisoners are not only used as "global guinea pigs" to test the advancement of criminal punishment technologies, as Zygmunt Bauman claims, but they are also used to satisfy the public's private rape fantasies and desires to be punished.

Epilogue
Global Effects of U.S. Discourses of Imprisonment

According to criminologist Michael Tonry, the current policies concerning crime and punishment are the most severe in U.S. history, and the harshest in the Western world; the United States is the only Western country that still uses the death penalty ("Crime" 3). Other scholars such as Nils Christie and Zygmunt Bauman have expressed concerns about the global effects of U.S. penal policies. Christie claims that, because of its status as *the* superpower in the world, the United States may influence penal legislation in other countries, and, therefore, the growth of imprisonment in the United States is a threat to the rest of the world as well (199). He emphasizes that the major threat that crime poses in modern societies like the United States is not crime itself, but the method of crime control—mass incarceration—because it has the potential to lead to "totalitarian developments"(16).

Bauman focuses on the totalitarian aspect of contemporary U.S. crime control as well, and compares current supermax prisons such as Pelican Bay to Nazi concentration camps. He writes:

> If the concentration camps served as laboratories of a totalitarian society, where the limits of human submission and serfdom were explored, and if the Panopticon-style workhouses served as the laboratories of industrial society, where the limits of routinization of human action were experimented with—the Pelican Bay prison is a laboratory of the "globalized" (or "planetary," in Alberto Melucci's terms) society, where the techniques of space-confinement of the rejects and the waste of globalization are tested and their limits are explored. (113)

The adverse effects of imprisonment that Christie and Bauman predict and criticize—the totalitarian developments and the dehumanization of prisoners as lab rats and global waste—serve as a major focal point of contemporary American prison narratives. The contemporary futuristic prison film extrapolates the evolution of the global business-oriented management of privatized prisons in which inmates are exploited as a free work force for building more prisons or as raw material for cyborg development; prison autobiography is likewise concerned with the dehumanizing effects of imprisonment; and the prison novel shows how prisoners primarily function as human waste—or as the American national other—that makes possible for the rest of American society to define itself in terms of that which it is not.

By focusing on these concerns, contemporary American prison narratives demonstrate that the problem of incarceration is an issue of human rights. By focusing on the dehumanizing storage of human beings as global waste, by depicting the development of the criminal justice system as penalizing machinery that criminalizes people for expressing fundamental human needs such as procreation and sexuality, and by displaying privatized international prisons as spaces where the Geneva Convention no longer applies, prison narratives represent incarceration as an human rights issue rather than as an issue relevant only to a marginal section of the population. International non-governmental organizations such as Human Rights Watch include the "prison project" on their agendas and thus demarginalize the institution of prison as merely a concern of "criminals" who deserve what they get.[1]

Michael Tonry, focusing on the embedded racism within the ideology of imprisonment, also defines incarceration as an issue of human rights. He writes that crime control has been at the center of partisan political agendas in the United States since the late 1960s when Republican presidential candidate Barry Goldwater campaigned using a "crime in the streets" rhetoric ("Crime" 3). As an example of the racist agendas in disguise embedded in tough-on-crime rhetoric, Tonry cites how George Prescott Bush used the "blackened" picture of convicted rapist and murderer Willie Horton in his successful 1988 presidential campaign to "remind" white voters that "blacks are disproportionately involved in violent crime [by conjuring] up the inflammatory image of a black man raping a white woman" (4).

The fact that images of criminals are used to promote presidential campaigns, while "systematic knowledge [about crime control and its effects] becomes irrelevant" in political arenas, signifies that crime and criminal identities are important to American culture at the level of the symbolic, if not at the level of the "real" (Tonry, "Crime" 6). The fantasy of the criminal, which embraces racist and homophobic ideologies, functions as a social and cultural referent with multiple meanings that are read and reproduced in the "global" context of crime.

I close my study, therefore, by briefly addressing the problematics of the import of U.S. discursive practices and ideologies of incarceration and criminality, and not merely the criminological implications of U.S. policies. Europeans, for instance, are proud of *not* embracing the traditional U.S. values and ideologies—and yet they readily consume everything "American." One can buy a Big Mac in the remotest of European villages, people fluently express their dismay by using the "international," "Oh, shit!," and Europeans do not bother to translate movie titles any longer—*Die Hard* is *Die Hard* in any language. There are also anecdotes about individuals who represent themselves in court and attempt to apply the practices learned from U.S. television shows: for instance, one defendant requested to be released on bail, without realizing that the bail bond system implemented on *Law & Order* did not apply in Finnish courtrooms.

That the public mind is more aware of crime and punishment as it is represented in U.S. courtroom dramas than it is of actual practices in various countries demonstrates the power of cultural import. The U.S. discourses of crime and criminality have permeated—practically unnoticed—other national cultural discourses and are considered to be more acceptable than the much more thoroughly critiqued ideology of America policing the world. The media images of crime and punishment in the United States have already had a fundamental, and perhaps lasting, impact on the conceptions of criminality in the rest of the Western world.

Adopted American ideologies of criminality have been recycled as normalized in cultural spaces in which they do not seem to belong. These alien ideologies not only represent discourses of harsh punishments and mass imprisonment, but also ideas reflecting the racist and homophobic discursive practices of incarceration in the United States. The seeping of discursive practices into new cultural spaces offers opportunities for analyzing a phenomenon in the making. In the Swedish author Åke Edwardson's detective novel, an ex-cop and three skinheads discuss the possibility of one of the young men going to prison, and they raise the question of what prison is like in today's Sweden. The answer demonstrates the power of the import of U.S. prison iconography: "Det är detsamma som att bli knullad I röven av negrer!"— "It's the same as being fucked in the ass by niggers!"(141).

Notes

NOTES TO THE INTRODUCTION

1. Throughout my work I use the terms "inmate" and "prisoner" interchangeably. Recently the media, following the practice of the criminal justice system, has started using the term "offender," apparently to include people who are not necessarily incarcerated, but under the supervision of the justice system—for example, on parole.

2. Starting from September 13, 2001, Santa Barbara County Sheriff, for instance, has organized public guided tours in the Santa Barbara County Jail Main Facility for people who want "to learn more about Custody Operations" (Santa Barbara). Visitors are subject to background checks to insure that they have no outstanding warrants. Judging by the rather strict dress code, the Jail is mainly expecting male visitors. The visitors must wear "conservative casual business apparel, slacks and shirt with comfortable walking shoes" (Santa Barbara). Also Nathan McCall, in his autobiography *Makes Me Wanna Holler,* writes about a "citizens' tour" of the prison where he served his sentence in about the year 1977 (216).

3. U.S. Department of Justice, Bureau of Justice Statistics, Prison Statistics on June 30, 2001. http://wwww.ojp.usdoj.gov/bjs/prisons.htm.

4. *Sourcebook of Criminal Justice Statistics 2000,* page 488. Table 6.1. Adults on probation, in jail or prison, and on parole. <http://www.Albany.edu/sorucebook/1995/ pdf/t61.pdf> 4–28–2002. Also the number of minors in adult prisons has more than doubled between 1985 and 1997, from 3,400 to 7,400, according to "Juvenile Court Statistics," a February 2000 report from the U.S. Bureau of Justice Statistics (Dennis Vol. 25, No. 4, 7).

5. Dennis, Douglas (ed.), *The Angolite,* News Briefs, July/August 1999, Vol. 24, No. 4, 9.

6. U.S. Department of Justice, Bureau of Justice Statistics, Prison Statistics on June 30, 2001 (1).

7. According to U.S. Department of Justice, Bureau of Justice Statistics Press Release of August 12, 2001, there were 91,612 women in state and federal prisons at the end of 2000. Since 1990 the number of female inmates has grown 108 percent, compared to male inmates by 77 percent (2).

8. See, for example, Eric Lichtblau's "Crime Down for 8th Year, FBI Reports" in the *LA Times* and Douglas Dennis' "Crime Drops Again" in *The Angolite.*

9. I have narrowed my study to prison narratives—written both by inmates and non-inmates—exploring imprisonment on U.S. soil. I have excluded, for example, prisoner-of-war narratives. I make only passing reference to poetry and films other than science fiction. Some of the excellent texts that I do not discuss, but that deserve attention as major prison narratives include plays such as Manuel Puig's *Kiss of the Spider Woman,* Miguel Piñero's *Short Eyes,* and Luis Valdez's *Zoot Suit;* the Native American writer Leonard Peltier's *Prison Writings: My Life Is My Sun Dance,* which includes both prose narrative and poetry; and Floyd Salas' autobiographical novel *Tattoo the Wicked Rose.* There are also a host of texts written by female inmates—mainly poetry and short stories—that are anthologized in H. Bruce Franklin's *Prison Writing in 20th-Century America* and Bell Gale Chevigny's *Doing Time: 25 Years of Prison Writing.* Octavia E. Butler's science fiction novel, *Dawn: Xenogenesis,* is a prison narrative that focuses on humans who survived a nuclear holocaust imprisoned by aliens from outer space for procreative purposes. Also two interesting collections of photographs focus on prisons, Ken Light's *Texas Death Row* and Bruce Jackson's *Killing Time: Life in the Arkansas Penitentiary.*

10. The disparity between the representations of criminal identities by authoritative sources and inmates themselves can also be analyzed in the light of what Carl Gutiérrez-Jones discusses as "a pattern of competing literacies" in crime-related discourses (1). In *Critical Race Narratives* (2001), with reference to the Rodney King and Amadou Diallo cases, Gutiérrez-Jones writes that "[t]o an important extent minorities and whites are reading race as well as racism differently" (1–2).

11. Tim Willocks is a British author, but his novel is set in the United States.

12. Stallybrass and White claim that "what is *socially* peripheral is so frequently *symbolically* central (like long hair in the 1960s)" (5).

13. Nils Christie's *Crime Control as Industry: Towards GULAGS, Western Style* (1994) focuses on criminality and imprisonment from a global perspective, and brings together a large amount of specific and analytical material ranging from Christie's theorization about the reasons for the increase of criminal behavior in modern world to his case study on the United States as a cautionary tale about policies of imprisonment gone awry.

14. For a discussion on high-tech prisons see Zygmunt Bauman's *Globalization: The Human Consequences* (106–113), in which he criticizes "post-correction age prisons" as "factories of immobility" (113, 106).

15. See Joseph T. Hallinan's *Going Up the River: Travels in a Prison Nation* for a discussion on work programs (143–154) and privatization of prisons (159, 163–185). Privatization is also criticized by Nils Christie in *Crime Control as Industry* (101–105), and Christian Parenti in *Lockdown America: Police and Prisons in the Age of Crisis* (221–225).

16. *Scientific American* also states, for example, that 68 percent of "death-penalty sentences [were] found to have serious error [and therefore resulted in] subsequent appeals" and that the age of mistakenly executed since 1900 is "at least 23" (16). About the ineffectiveness of incarceration, see Marc Mauer's *Race to Incarcerate* (191–194), and *Young Black Men and the Criminal Justice System: A Growing National Problem.*

17. In the section, "Money in slaves," Christie specifically focuses on prison conditions in Soviet Union and in China (73).

18. Mauer writes, for example, that in 1991 six percent of state inmates had not completed high school, 53 percent "earned less than $10,000 in the year prior to their incarceration," and that "nearly one half were either unemployed or working only part-time prior to their arrest" (162–163).

19. See, for instance, Angela Davis' "Masked Racism: Reflections on the Prison Industrial Complex" and "Race and Criminalization: Black Americans and the Punishment Industry," and Marc Mauer's *Race to Incarcerate.*

20. The data appears in Marc Mauer's "Black and the System" (28), which cites "various reports of the U.S. Bureau of Justice Statistics" (38).

21. Edward Bunker's autobiography, *Education of a Felon: A Memoir* (2000), reflects blatantly racist notions of black-white relationships in prison. In Chapter Fourteen, entitled "Prison Race War," Bunker outlines events that, according to him, represent a war between black and white inmates. The chapter is strangely unrelated to the rest of the autobiography in that it mostly describes events—such as George Jackson's trial—that Bunker himself did not witness and that it is separated from the rest of the narrative at the end of the book, which also marks a break in the temporal flow of the text. Throughout his narrative, Bunker comments that he "gets along with Chicanos" and that he is not "a racist." Yet, he writes, for example, "black racism is perhaps more virulent than white racism. Someone had once told me, 'When we're racists, we ['whites'] just want to stay away from 'em. When they're racists, they want to kill us.' It was true: black racists wanted revenge; white racists wanted segregation" (272).

22. See, for instance Kobena Mercer's *Welcome to the Jungle,* particularly Chapter Six on racial fetishism in Robert Mapplethorpe's photographs (171–219), and Richard Dyer's "The White Man's Muscles," in which he writes that Paul Robeson, "the first major African American acting star . . . appeared torso-naked or more for large sections in nearly all his films, on a scale unimaginable with while male stars" (262).

23. See also Charles Bright's *The Powers that Punish,* which he characterizes as a study of "the prison as a site of power in modern society" (1). He claims, for instance, that "the constitution of the political sphere is also the constitution of the disciplinary order inside the prison" (1).

24. See Douglas Dennis' account of the report of the National Commission on the Causes and Prevention of Violence in *The Angolite,* News Briefs, Vol. 25, No. 5, 5.

NOTES TO CHAPTER ONE

1. Other recent movies representing the futuristic prison film include *Escape from New York* (1981), *Blade Runner* (1982), *Star Trek VI: The Undiscovered Country* (1991), *Alien 3* (1992), *Demolition Man* (1993), *Escape from LA* (1996), and *Face/Off* (1997).

2. For more about longer and mandatory sentencing, see Kevin R. Reitz, "Sentencing" in *The Handbook of Crime and Punishment* (542–562) and Michael Tonry's introduction, "Crime and Punishment in America," to *The Handbook of Crime and Punishment,* which argues that prison sentences have grown longer due to "determinate" sentencing, to "truth-in-sentencing laws under which people convicted of selected violent crimes must serve at least 85 percent of the announced prison sentence," and to "laws requiring mandatory minimum sentences for drug and violent crimes, including in many states three-strike-laws that require life or very long sentences following the third conviction" (8–9).

3. For a discussion of political prisons and prisoners in the United States, see Ward Churchill and J.J. Vander Wall's (eds.) *Cages of Steel: The Politics of Imprisonment in the United States* (1992).

4. Marco Brambilla's *Demolition Man* (1993) is an exception to the dystopic views of crime in the future. In the utopian present of this film there is no crime, so the "new" crime is the violent crime such as murder.

5. Co-ed prisons—prisons where male and female inmates are "present and in interaction" (Mahan 134)—have been experimented and studied, particularly in the 1970s. One of these studies is Sue Mahan's study in the STAR unit at the Federal Correctional Institution—Fort Worth, Texas (published in *Corrections Today* in 1986). All interviewees were male inmates (136). Interestingly, Mahan speaks about "sexually integrated institutions," although sexual contact is strictly prohibited in these institutions (136, 138). The major positive result of these experiments is that "violence [was] all but eliminated" (165). The disadvantage of these experiments is the need for the increased monitoring of inmate behavior: "security efforts prohibiting sexual contact limit the number of staff members available for handling the serious living problems inmates experience" (164). From the inmates' point of view the prohibition of sexual contact is highly frustrating (140).

    See also, Hefferman, Esther, and Elizabeth Krippel, "A Coed Prison." *Justice and Corrections,* ed. by N. Johnson and L. Savitz. New York: John Wiley and Sons, 1978. Most studies focusing on coed prisons can be found in the areas of medicine and psychology. See, for example, Braithwaite, Ronald L. *Prisons and AIDS : A Public Health Challenge.* San Francisco: Jossey-Bass Publishers, 1996. The Jossey-Bass Health Series; Leukefeld, Carl G. and Frank M. Tims (eds.). *Drug Abuse Treatment in Prisons and Jails.* Rockville, MD: U.S. Dept. of Health and Human Services, Public Health Service, Alcohol, Drug Abuse, and Mental Health Administration, National Institute on Drug Abuse ; Washington, 1992. DHHS publication No. (ADM) 92–1884, National Institute on

Drug Abuse research monograph series, v.118; and Ostfeld, Adrian M. et al. *Stress, Crowding, and Blood Pressure in Prison.* Hillsdale, N.J.: L. Erlbaum Associates, 1987. Environment and Health Series.

6. Stephanie Rothman's *Terminal Island* (1973), which seems to be a major inspiration for later futuristic island-penitentiary films—for Campbell's *No Escape*, in particular—is set in the California of the near future. Capital punishment has been abolished in California and, instead, the new California penal code declares the prisoners in San Bruno Maximum Security Prison to be "legally dead." The concept that it is economically more feasible for the government to exile prisoners than to execute them also appears in John Carpenter's *Escape from New York* (where an option to prison is cremation, though) and *Escape from L.A.*

7. An exception to defining "global" as the United States is *Star Trek VI: The Undiscovered Country* (1991) directed by Nicholas Meyer, in which the prisoners speak different languages and recognize that they need an interpreter.

8. John Woo's *Face/Off* (1997) also addresses how prisoners of the future do no have civil or human rights, and its language is explicit. When the FBI Special Agent Sean Archer (John Travolta) enters the high-tech island prison as an inmate (mistakenly thought to be a terrorist using biological weapons), he is promptly told that he is a "citizen of nowhere," that the Geneva Contract no longer applies, and that Amnesty International does not know that the prison exists. Also, the current "three-strikes" laws have evolved into "two-strikes" laws. This prison has no visual control devices, but a "bio-magnetic field" monitors the movements of the prisoners.

9. Jesse Jackson (among others) claims that the United States already is in a situation that shames the nation in the eyes of the international community. In "The Crime of Punishment Taints All of America" (*LA Times,* Jan 9, 2000) he critiques the "locking [of] nonviolent offenders in prisons with the worst conditions that provide the least treatment" (M6).

10. Stern is specifically referring to advertisements in *Corrections Today,* a magazine for and about correctional institutions.

11. Also in *Terminal Island*, Dr. Norman Milford (Tom Selleck) is offered a new trial, in which he would probably be acquitted, but he decides to stay in order to continue living on the prison-turned-into-a-paradise San Bruno island after the "real" criminals had been eliminated. In *Escape from New York* and *Escape from LA*, "Snake" Pliskin (Kurt Russell) manages to escape after having solved the problem the government sent him to solve in the cities that had been turned into prisons. In *Demolition Man*, Spartan (Sylvester Stallone) escapes not only from having been deep-frozen in a California cryo-penitentiary, but also from his black arch-enemy, Simon Phoenix (Wesley Snipes), who is about to destroy the 2011 Santa Barbara-Los Angeles-San Diego Metroplex.

    The tendency of the white man to escape, and the non-white man either stay behind or be annihilated during his escape, is also typical of "historical" prison films: in *The Shawshank Redemption* (1994), for instance, the white male hero, Andy Dufresne (Tim Robbins) laboriously escapes, while his African American sidekick, "Red" Redding (Morgan Freeman), stays to complete his sentence.

12. Also "Snake" Pliskin has a military background and Spartan is an ex-police officer.

13. The black-white contrast becomes noticeable, in part, because there are so few non-white characters in these films. Interestingly, these films imagine a future with a primarily white prison population.

14. George Lipsitz discusses "generic representations," in particular, when he writes that "Hollywood westerns, war movies, detective stories, melodramas, and action/adventure films often rely on racial imagery, underscoring the heroism of white males by depicting them as defenders of women and children against predatory Indians, Asians, blacks and Mexicans"(*American* 186).

15. Chela Sandoval discusses cyborg representations as drawing from race discourse and theory. In *Methodology of the Oppressed* and in "New Sciences: Cyborg Feminism and the Methodology of the Oppressed," she writes, "colonized people of the Americas have already developed the cyborg skills required for survival under techno-human conditions," and "theorists of globalization engage with the introduction of an oppositional 'cyborg' politics as if these politics have emerged with the advent of electronic technology alone" (248).

16. A film that takes the issue of reproduction controlled by the institution of prison even further is Volker Schlöndorff's *The Handmaid's Tale* (1990), which projects a future where rightwing tyranny and religious intolerance result in the takeover of the reproductive rights of female prisoners at a time when female fertility has become extremely rare. Fertile female prisoners are placed to live with wealthy childless couples, be impregnated and bear a child for them. The wives of the powerful men of "The Republic of Gilead," like the female prisoners, are violated through their forced participation in the impregnation "ceremony," or rape.

17. In Richard Herley's novel, *The Penal Colony* (1989)—on which *No Escape* is based—homosexuality is the only act *not* tolerated on the prison island off the British coast (108). The reason for the prohibitive rule is the AIDS scare (108).

18. See, for example, Jeff Barnard's "Prison Riot," ABCNews.com at http://abcnews.go.com/sections/us/dailynews/prisonriot000224.html> 2–24–2001 and "Thirteen inmates shot, one killed, by guards in prison riot," ABCNews.com at <http://abcnews.go.com/wire/us/ap20000224_554.html> 2–24–2001.

NOTES TO CHAPTER TWO

1. For example, *Stop Prisoner Rape* expresses the view that the act of rape is non-sexual by stating that "rape is a crime of power which cannot alter the victim's masculinity or sexual orientation," and, more indirectly, "rape is frequently used worldwide by administrations against political prisoners" (1–2). *Life Sentences* claims that the "act of rape in the ultramasculine world of prison . . . is not sexual," although the long-term homosexual

relationships that ensue (often after the feminized victim has been raped) "will be sexual in nature as well as in form" (75, 82).

2. See the *Sourcebook of Criminal Justice Statistics 1999,* page 484. http://www.albany.edu/sourcebook/1995/pdf/t62.pdf> Table 6.2 Estimated number of adults under correctional supervision. June 28, 2001. "Under correctional supervision" refers to people in "State and Federal prisons, in local jails, on State and Federal probation, parole, and supervised release." Source: U.S. Department of Justice, Bureau of Justice Statistics, *Correctional Population in the United States, 1995,* NCJ-163916, Tables 1.3 and 1.4; *1997,* NCJ-177613, Tables 1.3 and 1.4 (Washington DC: U.S. Department of Justice). The disproportionate number of African Americans in prisons also applies to juvenile facilities: in Alameda County (Oakland and surrounding cities in northern California), for example, African Americans make up 60 percent of the incarcerated juveniles, while the percentage of black population in Alameda County is only 17 percent (MIM).

3. While Dr. Martin Luther King, Jr.'s "Letter from a Birmingham Jail" is not "autobiographical" in the traditional sense, it must be mentioned as one of the central texts of African American prison writing.

4. The main primary recipient and audience for most of George Jackson's prison letters, posthumously published as *Soledad Brother,* was his immediate family; Jackson himself did not make the decision to become a published prison writer.

5. In *Black Autobiography in America* (1974), Stephen Butterfield uses Ellison's *Invisible Man* to metaphorize the African American prison autobiography:

> The problem faced by the autobiographies of the "black revolution" is how to come forth from the tomb. In the case of convict writers like Cleaver and Jackson, the image applies in a quite literal sense; locked behind prison walls, whose function is to keep the invisible man invisible in white society so that its crimes will not be exposed to the light, how is the self to reach beyond the bars, to join hands with others in the same tomb and roll away the stone? (218)

6. Mumia Abu-Jamal writes in "Caged and Celibate" that only seven state jurisdictions "provide some degree of conjugal visitation": California, Connecticut, Minnesota, Mississippi, New York, South Carolina, and Washington (139). He also states, referring to George H. Gallup's *The Gallup Report,* report # 200 (1982), that the "American public strongly supported conjugal/family visitation" (140).

7. I refer to Judith Butler's Introduction to *Erotic Welfare* that succinctly draws together the various strands of Singer's manuscript, which she herself was not able to complete before her death.

8. Various genres of prison narratives tend to represent the African American males as the aggressive rapists. *Life Sentences* presents these statistics,

based on a study in the Philadelphia jails: 56 percent of the rapes were black-on-white, 29 percent black-on-black, and 15 percent white-on-white. They also mention another study, conducted in Connecticut's reformatories, where "the homosexual rapes . . . were usually blacks raping white boys for power and revenge" (92–93). See also Lynne Segal's *Slow Motion,* 247.

9. According to a "News Briefs" item titled, "Internet Wars" published in *The Angolite,* "Since no American prison allows prisoners direct access to the Internet, according to the *New York Times,* convicts utilize relatives or third parties to tell their stories. Some death-row prisoners [like Mumia Abu-Jamal] have web sites to champion their causes" (Dennis, "Internet" 10–11). The item also states that

> . . . officials in New York and Arizona enacted policies of laws forbidding prisoners to use third-party Internet services. California, Washington and other states are considering similar measures. Janet McGrath, a Republican state legislator who sponsored the New York law . . . said it galled the families of victims to see the smiling faces of criminals who claim they are innocent. "The Internet allows these people to distort history," she said. "It's a way of further victimizing the victim" . . . In the view of legal experts, laws like these cannot escape the Constitution. "It clearly impinges on an inmate's First Amendment right to communicate," said Eleanor Eisenberg, executive director of the Arizona ACLU. "It also chills the rights of third parties who have committed no crimes" (Dennis, "Internet" 10–11).

10. The *LA Times* reports that "Missouri Atty. Gen. Jay Nixon has sued [Benetton] for fraud, alleging that the company's representatives masqueraded as journalists to gain access to inmates—then used that access to help them sell sweaters" (Simon, A5). Sears also started a dispute with Benetton by pulling its contract "after taking heat from customers over ads." Sears said that the "advertising campaign was inconsistent with what Sears has come to stand for" ("Sears" 1).

11. Roger Rosenblatt, in "Black Autobiography: Life as the Death Weapon," claims that "all autobiography is minority autobiography" and that autobiography is "the least reliable of genres" because an autobiographical text focuses on an individual life, narrated by himself or herself (169).

12. John Paul Eakin discusses the idea of an autobiographer "as a man with 'a completed sense of his own life'" as a fiction. He cites Alex Haley's epilogue to Malcolm X's autobiography and claims that this is particularly obvious in Malcolm X's case, although Haley seems to want to paint a different picture. Eakin quotes Malcolm X: "I'm a man enough to tell you that I can't put my finger on exactly what my philosophy is now, but I'm flexible" (428). The sense of flexibility signals for Eakin the "fictive nature" of Malcolm X's "final testamentary" as Haley wants to represent it (Eakin, cited

in James Olney's *Autobiography: Essays Theoretical and Critical,* 182–183).

13.   See also Sidonie Smith's *Where I'm Bound* (1974), in which she notes,

> In a sense, Cleaver's is no conventional autobiography. He offers no facts about his background, family, youth and so on. But *Soul on Ice* joins such recent autobiographical writings as George Jackson's *Soledad Brother* and LeRoi Jones' *Home* among others, writings that are not so much histories of individuals as they are social analyses of American racism. (119)

14.   Chester Himes who is well known as a "convict" writer—most notably for his prison novel, *Cast the First Stone* (1952)—discusses his prison experience of "seven and a half years" only within six pages (*The Quality of Hurt: The Autobiography of Chester Himes* 61). He explains his reticence by saying that, "[n]othing happened in prison that [he] had not already encountered in outside life" (61).

15.   See also Paul John Eakin's *Touching the World: Reference in Autobiography* (1992), in which he discusses the concept of collaborative autobiography in the work of Philippe Lejeune (with reference to "The Autobiography of Those") and William L. Andrews (*To Tell a Free Story: The First Century of Afro-American Autobiography, 1760–1865*). Eakin points out, for example, that, when ex-slaves narrated their stories to their white amanuenses,

> ... the narratives were predictably targeted to reassure the middle-class sensibilities of the white reader, especially with regard to the fugitives' demonstrated potential to rebel against the authority of Southern white masters. White control of the instruments of public expression could effect a systematic repression of the violent anger and bitterness at the core of the black self ... (88).

Eakin also briefly discusses how the involvement of an "intermediary" creates a sense of ambiguities and ironies, to the extent that " the system of communication in question serves to promote the values and ideology of the dominant (literate) class" (88–89). He writes that as "Andrews and Lejeune demonstrate, collaborative autobiography offers a rich opportunity to explore the play of power and politics beneath the deceptive surface of first-person discourse with its rhetorical structure of self-authorization" (89). For a discussion of recent collaborative black autobiographies, see Albert E. Stone's *Autobiographical Occasions and Original Acts: Versions of American Identity from Henry Adams to Nate Shaw* (1982). Stone analyzes, for example, Malcolm X's autobiography as "a unique blend of oral social history and spiritual confession" that combines the characteristics of a memoir, "testament, polemic, apology, and eventually a searingly honest baring of the inner self" (250).

16. According to H. Bruce Franklin's *Prison Writing in 20th-century America,* all prison narratives spawn from slave work songs. See also David M. Oshinsky's *"Worse Than Slavery": Parchman farm and the Ordeal of Jim Crow Justice,* and John Edgar Wideman's "Introduction" to Abu-Jamal's *Live from Death Row* in which he discusses the best-selling black "up-from-the-depths" autobiography and biography as "neoslave narratives" (xxix).

17. Antonio Gramsci makes a similar statement in *Selections from Cultural Writings:*

> Autobiographies are often an act of pride: one believes one's own life is worth being narrated because it is "original," different from others, etc. Autobiography can be conceived "politically." One knows that one's life is similar to that of a thousand others, but through "chance" it has had opportunities that the thousand others in reality could not or did not have. By narrating it, one creates this possibility, suggests the process, indicates the opening. Autobiography therefore replaces the "political" or "philosophical essay": it describes in action what otherwise is deduced logically. Autobiography certainly has a great historical value in that it shows life in action and not just as written laws or dominant moral principles say it should be. (132)

18. For a discussion of black masculinity in contemporary popular imagination, see Herman Gray's "Black Masculinity and Visual Culture." In addition to the focus on visual culture, Gray discusses masculinities in "black" music, jazz, blues, and rap lyrics.

19. Several authors comment on the rapist's sexuality as heterosexual. For an interesting discussion of this topic, see Wilbert Rideau and Ron Wikberg's *Life Sentences* (81–95).

20. Billy Hayes, in *Midnight Express,* implies the sameness of heterosexuality and homosexuality when he discusses his relationship with another male prisoner, Arne, who comments on their homosexual exchange: "It's all right Willie. It's only love" (174).

21. Kendall Thomas discusses homophobia in the black community in terms of James Baldwin's presumed homosexuality or bisexuality and the difficulty of its acceptance in the community and its representation in literature. He also quotes the "gansta-rapper" Ice-Cube who says, "true niggers ain't gay" (59).

22. The chapter, "The Sexual Jungle," won the 1980 George Polk Award and was cited "as the most definitive work on the subject" of prison sexuality (Rideau 107).

23. Wilbert Rideau and Ron Wikberg's *Life Sentences* also points out that control of sexual acts "does not halt sexual relations; it only effects a change of

form" (84). As an example of change of form the authors mention the shift from anal intercourse to fellatio, because it "does not require the removal of clothing, so it is quicker and easier to conceal from authorities" (84).

24. The Harvard University criminologist, Dr. James Gilligan, claims, for instance, that some prison officials "quietly permit rape as a way to control the population" and that rapists may be "given a bribe of a reward to cooperate with the prison authorities" (Harris, "Nowhere"). See also Wilbert Rideau and Ron Wikberg's *Life Sentences* (89–94) and Christian Parenti's *Lockdown America: Police and Prisons in the Age of Crisis,* in which he argues that rape is used as a "semi-official disciplinary tool" (182–210).

25. Rap music is a subgenre of African American prison autobiography that primarily focuses on police brutality and the racial injustice in the U.S. criminal justice system. This form of prison autobiography deserves an in depth discussion in another context. See Tricia Rose's *Black Noise* and Crispin Sartwell's "Rap Music and the Uses of Stereotype" in *Act Like You Know* (159–196).

26. For a discussion on the position of a known sex offender in prison, see the "Rapo" section in Robert Ellis Gordon's *The Funhouse Mirror,* 23–37.

27. Since the focus of my study is McCall's prisoner identity, I do not discuss his relationships with women outside prison. The only woman McCall meets in prison, the teacher Mrs. Pinkney, emasculates him by making a "fool of him" (200), and, thus, it seems that McCall's relationship with Mrs. Pinkney was more threatening to his masculinity than his contacts with gay men and rapists.

28. According to Sidonie Smith in *Where I'm Bound,* Cleaver's take on sexuality and politics is different from contemporary prison autobiographers:

> Significantly, Cleaver links rebellion against American society, or rather American capitalism, with a "ruthless attitude toward white women." For Cleaver, slavery to the white woman symbolizes his enslavement to capitalism: politics and sexual relationships become the two sides of the same coin. Hence, upon his release from prison, he deliberately chooses rape as a revolutionary act that embodies his new sense of liberation from the American system. (106, citing *Soul On Ice*)

NOTES TO CHAPTER THREE

1. Hallinan quotes a study conducted by team of U.S. Department of Justice experts headed by William G. Nagel, a former deputy superintendent in the New Jersey prison system.

2. See, for example, Michael Tonry's "Introduction: Crime and Punishment in America" in *The Handbook of Crime and Punishment* (ed. by Tonry, 1998) for a discussion of the correlation of race, gender, and criminality in terms of violent and non-violent crimes, including statistics from 1970–1995 (16–21). See also Weinstein and Cummins' "The Crime of

Punishment: Pelican Bay Maximum Security Prison" in *Criminal Injustice: Confronting the Prison Crisis* (ed. by Elihu Rosenblatt, 1996), a discussion of racial inequity in prisons claiming, for example, that California's African Americans and other minorities receive harsher treatment than whites at each stage in the justice system: "arrest, pre-trial hearing, conviction, sentencing, classification hearing during imprisonment, and parole hearing" (314).

3. George Lipsitz discusses the United States as based on hierarchies using "divide and conquer" strategies implemented by "people with power" (*American* 117). Lipsitz also points out, however, that these new divisions based on the logic of racism, sexism, homophobia, or class oppression "can also produce unexpected affiliations and alliances" (117–118). For example, "[a]ttacks of bilingual education and immigrant rights harm *both* Latinos and Asian Americans" (118).

4. In *City of Quartz: Excavating the Future in Los Angeles* (1990) Mike Davis discusses the urban space of Los Angeles with its fenced areas, armed guards, and surveillance cameras as an extension of prison-like architecture.

5. See, for example, Nathan Heard's *House of Slammers,* where kitchen jobs are the most sought after, and Suzanne Donovan's introduction to Ken Light's *Texas Death Row,* "Shadow Figures: A Portrait of Life on the Row," in which she discusses the system of employment in the section entitled "The Tiers of Death Row" (11–13).

6. See James B. Jacobs' discussion in *New Perspectives on Prisons and Imprisonment:* "In many prisons, officials explicitly consider race in making work and cell assignments in order to keep certain groups apart, or in some cases, to achieve racial balance. But most officials are frightened to admit that they act this way; they fear that the courts would find their practices unconstitutional" (82).

7. According to Tim Willocks' novel, *Green River Rising* (1994), "All the inmates on [cellblock] B were black. There was no official segregation policy but in an environment saturated with danger and fear men naturally drew together in tribal groups and in the interests of an uneasy peace, [Warden] Hobbes and his guards allowed it" (5). Although the excerpt verifies the racial organization of prisoners, the idea that the inmates are able to choose their cells contradicts other prison literature.

8. See, for example, Jerome Washington's "Afterword" to *Iron House,* in which he discusses his need to tell "the truth" about life in prison (158) despite the fact that his literary enterprise constantly caused him trouble within the institution and even led to a criminal investigation in which he was accused of being an informant planted in prison either by the Black Panthers or the Black Liberation Army in order to "foment riots throughout the entire prison system" (160). He was later acquitted.

9. See George Von der Muhll's "The Political Element in Literature," particularly page 30, in which Von der Muhll indirectly refers to Foucault and Gramsci and the concept of "ideological 'hegemony'": " . . . literature performs its most fundamental political task in exposing the contours of the overtly nonpolitical philosophies that limit perceptions of what is politically possible" (30).

10. Ernest Brawley, in his novel, *The Rap,* reports on the racial mix of a prison in a more metaphoric manner. In the opening of the novel, the narrator describes the scene where the new inmates' hair is being cut. Wasco Garland Weed's hair was falling on the floor, "mixing it up with the hundred other varieties of hair lying there in deep ratty piles on the floor: black, gray, red, brown, strawberry, curly, kinky, wavy, straight" (15).

11. In *American Social Fiction: James to Cozzens* (1964), Michael Millgate states that the "institutional novel" is a "direct response to the growth of vast bureaucratic institutions in every area of American life" (143). The institutions that Millgate discusses are military institutions, Hollywood and the motion-picture business, and universities and colleges (143), and the institutional novels that he focuses on include Irvin Shaw's *The Young Lions,* Norman Mailer's *The Naked and the Dead,* and Mary McCarthy's *The Groves of Academe.*

12. In *Prison Pictures from Hollywood: Plots, Critiques, Casts and Credits for 293 Theatrical and Made-For-Television Releases* (1991), James Robert Parish lists, as the title suggests, 293 prison films released up to 1989, while David R. Werner, in *Joint Images: An Annotated Bibliography of Prison Fiction* (1990), lists 134 titles up to 1989, roughly half of which are non-U.S. fiction. Werner calls his bibliography "An Idiosyncratic Collection" that attempts to "provide the broadest view of prison fiction possible" and therefore his criteria for what constitutes prison fiction is rather loose (ix). Within the category of prison fiction he includes works such as Jack Henry Abbott's *In the Belly of the Beast,* a drama based on Abbott's autobiographical text of the same title, and also several international works that are less clearly *prison* fiction—for example, Samuel Beckett's *Waiting for Godot,* John Milton's *Paradise Lost,* and Samuel Richardson's *Pamela.* In H. Bruce Franklin's *Prison Writing in 20th-Century America,* only five prison novelists are discussed: Malcolm Braly, Edward Bunker, Nathan Heard, Chester Himes, and Dannie Martin. In this extensive collection Franklin prioritizes poems as fictive prison writing.

13. John Bender's *Imagining the Penitentiary* (1987) compares the institution of the prison, or penitentiary, to the realist novel by metaphorizing the concept of narrative "transparency," and by focusing on the position of an individual in these "cultural systems" (211, 215). He writes,

> Both the realist novel and penitentiary pretend that character is autonomous, but in both cases invisible authority is organizing a mode of representation whose way of proceeding includes the premise, and fosters the illusion, that the consciousness they present is as free to shape circumstance as to be shaped by it . . . For [Bakhtin], the novel evades the hegemony of official culture. Conversely, I have shown the place of the realist novel in the dense array of modern culture: its narrative devices, like those of the penitentiary, place the individual on an entirely revised footing vis-à-vis authority. They redefine the way of being in the world. (212, 213)

14. Like Nathan Heard in *House of Slammers,* Edward Bunker appears to fictionalize this riot. In his novel, *The Animal Factory* (1977), set in San Quentin, the narrator claims that "the officials had deliberately turned a strike into a racial confrontation" (62). He also narrates that the conditions in the prison leading to the strike would not be publicly discussed, and that on the radio news the incident was reported as "a racial altercation between neo-Nazi white inmates and black militants" (65, 69). For another version of the events of the "Riot of '67," see Eric Cummins' *The Rise and Fall of California's Radical Prison Movement* (87–90).

15. See also James Massey's discussion of this aspect in Chester Himes' *Cast the First Stone* in *Doing Time in American Prisons: A Study of Modern Novels* (190–191).

16. See also Malcolm M. Klein's "Street Gangs"(in *The Handbook of Crime and Punishment,* ed. by Michael Tonry) in which he discusses how the concept of gangs affects the criminal justice system. He says, for example, that "law enforcement has combined with politicians to define gangs and gang crime in order to improve gang prosecutions and to apply heavier punishments specifically to gang members" (113).

17. For a discussion of Black Muslims in the California prison system, see Chapter Four of Eric Cummins' *The Rise and Fall of California's Radical Prison Movement,* "Taking the Yard, Freeing the Mind: The Black Muslims" (63–92). For another perspective on Black Muslim activity and its effects, see Joseph Hallinan's *Going Up the River* (25–28).

18. Hallinan refers to Bert Useem and Peter Kimball's *States of Siege: U.S. Prison Riots, 1971–1986* (10).

19. This approach could also be a reaction to accusations that correctional leniency has permitted gangs to thrive in prisons (Hallinan 96). Hallinan claims, however, that leniency is not the reason that gang activity has flourished in prison, but rather overcrowding that forces the mixing of strong and weak prisoners (96–98).

20. For a discussion of the history of a contemporary African American prison movement, see Sundiata Acoli's "A Brief History of the New Afrikan Prison Struggle (Parts 1 and 2)."

21. An exception might be Octavia E. Butler's science-fiction novel *Dawn* (1987), which narrates the incarceration of nuclear holocaust survivors in outer space.

NOTES TO CHAPTER FOUR

1. Benetton shocked the public earlier as well with its graphic ads featuring dying AIDS patients, and with ads displaying the idea of the "United Colors of Benetton" through the placement of different "colored" bodies next to each other, for instance. In *Disturbing Pleasures,* Henry Giroux writes that these kinds of images of racial harmony "render racial unity as a purely aesthetic category while eliminating racial conflict completely" (7). He also comments that an ad featuring a black and white male hand handcuffed to each other manifests "calculated and false equality," particularly because this

image, "given the legacy of white racism in [the United States, England, France, South Africa]," is likely to reproduce "the racist assumption that crime, turmoil, and lawlessness are essentially a black problem" (21).

2. This publication has no pagination.

3. For a more complete discussion of the subject, see Auli Ek's "'We, On Death Row': Advertising and Politics as Popular Culture."

4. I use the terms "gaze" and "look" as virtually synonymous in most of my text, and will note when I use "gaze" in a more specific sense—for example, in the sense that traditionally the male gaze is seen to define the female as an object of that gaze, as Laura Mulvey argues.

5. See, for example, David Lyon's *The Electronic Eye: The Rise of Surveillance Society* and *Surveillance Society: Monitoring Everyday Life,* and Reg Whitaker's *The End of Privacy.*

6. Reg Whitaker also points out that the act of surveillance is particularly typical of capitalist society—for the purposes of the state (for taxation, for example) and of private enterprise.

7. See also Gareth Palmer's "The new spectacle of crime" in which he discusses the production of "citizen subjectivity" in the context of television shows such as *Crimewatch, Crimebeat,* and *Cops.*

8. See David Lyon's discussion of "Personhood and Postmodernity" in *The Electronic Eye: The Rise of Surveillance Society.*

9. For more about the New Afrikan Nation see, for example, Acoli, Sundiata, *A Brief History of the New Afrikan Prison Struggle* at <http://www.global-africa.com/ Sundiata htm>, Paasewe, Khandi, Rev, *New Afrikan Independence Movement* at <http://www.netset.com/~khandi/pgrna1.htm>, and "Sanyika Shakur," an interview with Sanyika Shakur by N. Kurshan at <http://www-unix.oit.umass.edu/~kastor/fallprogram/fall-shakur.html>.

10. For images of prison tattoos, see Bruce Jackson's *Killing Time: Life in the Arkansas Penitentiary* (Ithaca, NY: Cornell University Press, 1977) and Ken Light's *Texas Death Row* (essay by Suzanne Donovan. Jackson: University Press of Mississippi, 1997).

11. See also Wiegman's "Feminism, 'The Boyz,' and Other Matters Regarding the Male" (173–193) in *Screening the Male: Exploring Masculinities in Hollywood Cinema* (ed. Steven Cohan and Ina Rae Hark, London and New York: Routledge, 1993).

12. Besides using expressions denoting metaphoric eyes, Cleaver specifically focuses on his own eyes and on the eyes of others; for instance in the vignette, "Eyes," he speaks about a woman who appreciated his "beautiful brown eyes," about his Muslim brother who called his eyes "the devil's eyes" because they are light brown, and about the "whites of *their* [the whites'] eyes" (39, 70).

13. The detailed description of his daily routines comes from a letter to his lawyer, Beverly Axelrod, with whom Cleaver has fallen in love.

14. Cleaver also discusses his problematic relationship with white women at some length. In the context of the pinup episode, he states that he was "shocked" because he realized that he actually did "prefer white girls over black" (21).

15. In my Writing 2 class, in the UCSB Writing Program, I assigned my students the topic of prison humor, and in their essays they offered the following observations: "One of the reasons for [the] light-hearted approach to jails and the death penalty is because the audience rarely relates to the criminal" (Allison Remple); "the vast majority of people have neither empathy or sympathy for inmates so [making fun of prisoners' pain] is an easy way to get a laugh without offending a crucial market segment" (Charles Thomas); and we laugh at prisoners because they represent "[the criminal justice] system [that] is seen as a joke"(Matthew Brothers). All of these comments reinforce the idea that the prisoner, as the "other," is therefore the acceptable butt of jokes.

NOTES TO THE EPILOGUE

1. See the *Human Rights Watch* website <http://www.hrw.org/about.html> and its report "Prisons in the United States of America" <http://www.hrw.org/advocacy/prisons/u-s.htm>.

Bibliography

Abbott, Jack Henry. *In the Belly of the Beast*. New York: Random House, 1981.

ABC News. Tonight with Peter Jennings. ABC. 2001.

Abu-Jamal, Mumia. "Caged and Celibate." *Prison Masculinities*. Eds. Don Sabo, Terry A. Kupers, and Willie London. Philadelphia: Temple University Press, 2001.

———. *Live from Death Row*. Introduction by John Edgar Wideman. New York: Avon Books, 1996.

Acoli, Sundiata. "A Brief History of the New Afrikan Prison Struggle (Parts 1 and 2)." 17 July 2001. <http://www.globalafrica.com/Sundiata.htm>.

Alien 3. Dir. David Fincher. Twentieth Century Fox Film Corp., 1992.

Ally McBeal. Fox. 2002.

Almaguer, Tomás. "Chicano Men: A Cartography of Homosexual Identity and Behavior." *The Lesbian and Gay Studies Reader*. Ed. Henry Abelove et al. New York: Routledge, 1993.

American History X. Dir. Tony Kaye. New Line Cinema, 1998.

American Me. Dir. James Edward Olmos. Universal Pictures, 1992.

America's Funniest Videos. ABC. 2002.

America's Most Wanted: America Fights Back. Fox. 2002.

Andrews, William, L. "African-American Autobiography Criticism: Retrospect and Prospect." *American Autobiography: Retrospect and Prospect*. Ed. Paul John Eakin. Wisconsin Studies in American Autobiography. Madison: University of Wisconsin Press, 1991. 195–215.

The Angolite: The Prison News Magazine. Louisiana State Penitentiary.

Bad Girls Dormitory. Dir. Tim Kincaid. Films Around the World, 1985.

Baker, Houston A., Jr. and Patricia Redmond, eds. *Afro-American Literary Study in the 1990s*. Chicago and London: University of Chicago Press, 1989.

Baldwin, James. *The Fire Next Time*. London: Michael Joseph, 1963.

———. *If Beale Street Could Talk*. New York: Dial Press, 1974.

Barnard, Jeff. "Prison Riot." *ABCNews.com* 24 Feb. 2001. <http://abcnews.go.com/sections/us/dailynews/prisonriot000224.html>.

Bauman, Zygmunt. *Globalization: The Human Consequences*. New York: Columbia University Press, 1998.

Bender, John. *Imagining the Penitentiary: Fiction and the Architecture of Mind in Eighteenth-century England*. Chicago and London: University of Chicago Press, 1987.

Benetton. *Press Release*. New York. 7 January 2000.

The Big Doll House. Dir. Jack Hill. New World, 1971.

The Birth of a Nation. Dir. D. W. Griffith. Allied Artists Classic Library, 1915.

Blade Runner. Dir. Ridley Scott. Warner Bros., 1982.

Blood In, Blood Out. Dir. Taylor Hackford. Hollywood Pictures Home Video, 1993.

Braithwaite, Ronald L. *Prisons and AIDS: A Public Health Challenge*. San Francisco: Jossey-Bass Publishers, 1996.

Braly, Malcolm. *On the Yard*. New York: Penguin, 1967.

Brawley, Ernest. *The Rap*. New York: Atheneum, 1974.

Bright, Charles. *The Powers that Punish: Prison and Politics in the Era of the "Big House," 1920–1955*. Ann Arbor: University of Michigan Press, 1996.

Brothers, Matthew. "Is the System a Joke in Today's Society?" Unpublished essay, 2002.

Bryant, Dorothy. *Prisoners*. Berkeley, CA: Ata Books, 1980.

Bunker, Edward. *The Animal Factory*. New York: Viking Press, 1977.

———. *Dog Eat Dog*. New York: St. Martin's Press, 1996.

———. *Education of a Felon: A Memoir*. New York: St. Martin's Press, 2000.

———. *No Beast So Fierce*. New York: Norton, 1973.

Bureau of Justice Statistics. Press Release. 12 Aug. 2001. 1 May 2002. <http://www.ojp.usdoj.gov/bjs/pub/press/p00pr.htm>.

———. Prison Statistics. U.S. Department of Justice. 30 June 2000. 22 April 2002. <http://www.ojp.usdoj.gov/bjs/prisons.htm>.

Butler, Judith. Introduction to Linda Singer's *Erotic Welfare: Sexual Theory and Politics in the Age of Epidemic*. Ed. and introduced by Judith Butler and Maureen MacGrogan. New York and London: Routledge, 1993.

Butler, Octavia E. *Dawn: Xenogenesis*. New York: Warner Books, 1988.

Butterfield, Stephen. *Black Autobiography in America*. Amherst: University of Massachusetts Press, 1974.

Caged Heat. Dir. Jonathan Demme. New World, 1974.

Cahill, Tom. Email to the author. 28 July 2001.

Carlson, L. Wayne. "Victims' Issues: An Inside View of Prison Life." *The Journal of Prisoners on Prisons*. Vol. 9, No. 2, 1998. 43–51.

Carter, Rubin. *The Sixteenth Round: From Number 1 Contender to # 45472*. New York: Viking Press, 1974.

Cast Away. Dir. Robert Zemeckis. Twentieth Century Fox Film Corp., 2000.

Chevigny, Bell Gale, ed. *Doing Time: 25 years of Prison Writing*. New York: Arcade Publishing, 1999.

Christie, Nils. *Crime Control as Industry: Towards GULAGS, Western Style*. Second and enlarged edition. London and New York: Routledge, 1994.

Churchill, Ward and J.J. Vander Wall, eds. *Cages of Steel: The Politics of Imprisonment in the United States*. Washington, D.C.: Maisonneuve Press, 1992.

Cleaver, Eldridge. *Soul on Ice*. 1968. New York: Bantam Doubleday Dell, 1992.

Conover, Ted. *Newjack*. New York and Toronto: Random House, 2000.

Corrections Today. American Correctional Association. College Park, MD.

"Crime and Punishment." Narr. Ted Koppel. *Nightline in Primetime*. ABC, 1998.

Cummins, Eric. *The Rise and Fall of California's Radical Prison Movement*. Stanford, CA: Stanford University Press, 1994.

Davidson, Theodore. *Chicano Prisoners: The Key to San Quentin.* Prospect Heights, Ill.: Waveland Press, 1974.

Davis, Angela Y. "Masked Racism: Reflections on the Prison Industrial Complex." *Rap Coalition.* 17 July 2001. <http://www.slavesnomore.bigstep.com/generic.html?pid=17>.

———. "Race and Criminalization: Black Americans and the Punishment Industry." *The House That Race Built: Black Americans, U.S. Terrain.* Ed. Wahneema Lubiano. New York: Pantheon, 1997.

———. "The Soledad Brothers." *The Black Scholar: Journal of Black Studies and Research.* Vol. 2, Nos. 8–9, April-May 1971. 2–7.

Davis, Mike. *City of Quartz: Excavating the Future in Los Angeles.* London and New York: Verso, 1990.

De Certeau, Michel. *The Practice of Everyday Life.* Trans. Steven F. Rendall. Berkeley and London: University of California Press, 1984.

Defoe, Daniel. *Robinson Crusoe.* 1844. New York: Knopf, 1992.

Demolition Man. Dir. Marco Brambilla. Warner Bros., 1993.

Dennis, Douglas, ed. "Bottoming Out." News Briefs. *The Angolite.* Vol. 25, No. 6. 6.

———. "Crime Drops Again." News Briefs. *The Angolite.* Vol. 25, No. 3. 5.

———. "A Federal Case." News Briefs. *The Angolite.* Vol. 25, No. 5. 5.

———. "Internet Wars." News Briefs. *The Angolite.* Vol. 25, No. 6. and Vol. 26, No 1. 10–11.

———. "Kids as Adults." News Briefs. *The Angolite.* Vol. 25, No. 4. 7.

———. News Briefs. *The Angolite.* Table: Prison Populations. Source: National Center on Institutions and Alternatives. Vol. 24, No. 4. 9.

———. News Briefs. *The Angolite.* Vol. 25, No. 5. 5.

Die Hard. Dir. John McTiernan. Twentieth Century Fox Film Corp., 1988.

Douglass, Frederick. From "My Bondage and My Freedom." 1855. *The Oxford Frederick Douglass Reader.* Ed. William L. Andrews. New York and Oxford: Oxford University Press, 1996. 164–222.

———. "Narrative of the Life of Frederick Douglass, An American Slave, Written by Himself." 1845. *The Oxford Frederick Douglass Reader.* Ed. William L. Andrews. New York and Oxford: Oxford University Press, 1996. 21–97.

Dyer, Richard. "The White Man's Muscles." *The Masculinity Studies Reader.* Eds. Rachel Adams and David Savran. Malden, Mass. and Oxford: Blackwell Publishers, 2002. 262–273.

Eakin, Paul John. *American Autobiography: Retrospect and Prospect.* Wisconsin Studies in American Autobiography. Madison: University of Wisconsin Press, 1991.

———. "Foreword" to Lejeune, Philippe. *On Autobiography.* Ed. Paul John Eakin. Trans. Katherine Leary. Theory and History of Literature, Vol. 52. Minneapolis: University of Minnesota Press, 1989.

———. *Touching the World: Reference in Autobiography.* Princeton, NJ: Princeton University Press, 1992.

Edwardson, Åke. *Till Allt Som Varit Dött.* Stockholm: Norstedts Förlag, 1995.

Ek, Auli. "'We, On Death Row': Advertising and Politics as Popular Culture." Unpublished article, 2000.

Escape from Alcatraz. Dir. Don Siegel. Paramount Pictures, 1979.

Escape from L.A. Dir. John Carpenter. Paramount Pictures, 1996.

Escape from New York. Dir. John Carpenter. AVCO Embassy Pictures, 1981.

Face/Off. Dir. John Woo. Paramount Pictures, 1997.

The Farm: Life Inside Angola Prison. Dir. Jonathan Stack and Liz Garbus. Gabriel Films, 1998.

Farr, Jory. "Prison Culture Proves Impossible to Lock Up." 17 July 2001. <http://www.press-enterprise.com/focus/prison/html/prison_culture.html>.

Fiske, John. *Media Matters: Race and Gender in U.S. Politics.* Minneapolis and London: University of Minnesota Press, 1996.

Fortress. Dir. Stuart Gordon. Dimension Films, 1993.

48 Hrs. Dir. Walter Hill. Paramount Pictures, 1982.

Foucault, Michel. *Discipline and Punish: The Birth of the Prison.* 1975. Translated from the French by Alan Sheridan. New York: Vintage, 1979.

———. "The Eye of Power." *Power/Knowledge: Selected Interviews and Other Writings.* Ed. Colin Gordon. New York: Pantheon Books, 1980.

———. *The Foucault Reader.* Ed. Paul Rabinow. New York: Pantheon Books, 1984.

———. *The History of Sexuality.* Volume I: An Introduction. Translated from the French by Robert Hurley. New York: Random House, 1978.

———. "The Subject and Power." *Michel Foucault: Beyond Structuralism and Hermeneutics.* Eds. Hubert Dreyfus and Paul Rabinow. Chicago: University of Chicago Press, 1982.

Franklin, H. Bruce, ed. *Prison Writing in 20th-Century America.* New York and London: Penguin, 1998.

Garfield, Bob. "The Colors of Exploitation: Benetton on Death Row." *Advertising Age.* V. 71, No. 2, 10 Jan 2000. 45.

Geismar, Maxwell. Introduction to Eldridge Cleaver's *Soul on Ice.* 1968. New York: Bantam Doubleday Dell, 1992.

Giroux, Henry, A. *Disturbing Pleasures: Learning Popular Culture.* New York and London: Routledge, 1994.

Goines, Donald. *White Man's Justice, Black Man's Grief.* Los Angeles: Holloway House Publishing Company, 1973.

Gordon, Colin. "Afterword." *Power/Knowledge: Selected Interviews and Other Writings.* Ed. Colin Gordon. New York: Pantheon Books, 1980.

Gordon, Robert Ellis and Inmates of the Washington Corrections System. *The Funhouse Mirror: Reflections on Prison.* Pullman, Washington: Washington State University Press, 2000.

Gramsci, Antonio. *Selections from Cultural Writings.* Ed. David Forgacs and Geoffrey Nowell-Smith. Trans. William Boelhower. Cambridge, Mass.: Harvard University Press, 1985.

Gray, Herman. "Black Masculinity and Visual Culture." 4 Oct. 2001. <http://muse.jhu.edu/quick_tour/18.2gray.html>.

The Green Mile. Dir. Frank Darabont. Warner Home Video, 1999.

Gutiérrez-Jones, Carl. *Critical Race Narratives: A Study of Race, Rhetoric, and Injury.* New York and London: New York University Press, 2001.

———. *Rethinking the Borderlands: Between Chicano Culture and Legal Discourse.* Berkeley and London: University of California Press, 1995.

Hall, Stuart. "Notes on Deconstructing 'the Popular.'" *People's History and Socialist Theory.* Ed. Raphael Samuel. London: Routledge and Kegan Paul, 1981. 227–240.

Hallinan, Joseph T. *Going Up the River: Travels in a Prison Nation.* New York: Random House, 2001.

The Handmaid's Tale. Dir. Volker Schlöndorff. Based on the novel of the same title by Margaret Atwood. Screenplay Harold Pinter. Cinecom Entertainment Group, Inc. Video. 1990.

Haraway, Donna J. *Simians, Cyborgs, and Women: The Reinvention of Nature.* New York: Routledge, 1991.

Harris, Dan. "Aftershock of Inmate Rape." *ABC World News Tonight.* 17 April 2001. <http://more.abcnews.go.com/sections/wnt/worldnewstonight/wnt010417_prisonrape2_feature.html>.

———. "Nowhere to Hide." *ABC World News Tonight.* 16 April 2001. <http://more.abcnews.go.com/sections/wnt/worldnewstonight/wnt010416_prisonrape1_feature.html>.

Hayes, Billy with William Hoffer. *Midnight Express.* New York: E. P. Dutton and Co., 1977.

Heard, Nathan C. *House of Slammers.* New York and London: Macmillan, 1983.

Hebdige, Dick. *Subculture: the Meaning of Style.* London and New York: Random House, 1987.

Hefferman, Esther and Elizabeth Krippel. "A Coed Prison." *Justice and Corrections.* Ed. N. Johnson and L. Savitz. New York: John Wiley and Sons, 1978.

Herley, Richard. *The Penal Colony.* New York: Routledge, 1989.

Himes, Chester. *Cast the First Stone.* New York: Coward-McCann, Inc., 1952.

———. *The Quality of Hurt: The Autobiography of Chester Himes.* Volume I. New York: Doubleday, 1972.

Human Rights Watch. <http://www.hrw.org/about.html> 13 June 2002.

Human Rights Watch. "No Escape: Male Rape in U.S. Prisons." <http://www.hrw.org/reports/2001/prison> 13 June 2002.

The Hurricane. Dir. Norman Jewison. Buena Vista International, 1999.

The Hurricane Carter Story. American Justice series. Video cassette. A&E Television Networks, 1999.

Jackson, Bruce. *Killing Time: Life in the Arkansas Penitentiary.* Ithaca, NY: Cornell University Press, 1977.

Jackson, George. *Soledad Brother: The Prison Letters of George Jackson.* 1970. Chicago: Lawrence Hill Books, 1994.

Jackson, Jesse. "The Crime of Punishment Taints All of America." *Los Angeles Times,* 9 Jan. 2000, Vol. CXIX, No. 37.

Jacobs, James B. *New Perspectives on Prisons and Imprisonment.* Ithaca, NY and London: Cornell University Press, 1983.

Jameson, Fredric. "Progress Versus Utopia; or, Can We Imagine the Future?" *Science Fiction Studies,* No. 27, Vol. 9, Part 2, July 1982. 147–158.

The Journal of Prisoners on Prisons. University of Ottawa. Ottawa, Ontario, Canada.

King, Martin Luther, Jr. "Letter from a Birmingham Jail." *I Have a Dream: Writings and Speeches that Changed the World*. Ed. James Melvin Washington. San Francisco: Harper, 1986.

King, Stephen. *The Green Mile*. New York: Pocket Books, 1999.

———. "Rita Hayworth and the Shawshank Redemption." *Different Seasons*. London and New York: Penguin, 1982.

Klein, Malcolm M. "Street Gangs." *The Handbook of Crime and Punishment*. Ed. Michael Tonry. New York and Oxford: Oxford University Press, 1998. 111–132.

Lane, Alycee. "Black Bodies/Gay Bodies: the Politics of Race in the Gay/Military Battle." *Callaloo*. Fall 1994, V. 17, N. 4, p. 1074(15).

Law & Order. NBC. 2002.

Lejeune, Philippe. *On Autobiography*. Edited and with a foreword by Paul John Eakin. Trans. Katherine Leary. Theory and History of Literature, Vol. 52. Minneapolis: University of Minnesota Press, 1989.

Leukefeld, Carl G. and Frank M. Tims, eds. *Drug Abuse Treatment in Prisons and Jails*. DHHS publication No. (ADM) 92–1884, National Institute on Drug Abuse research monograph series, v. 118. Rockville, MD: U.S. Dept. of Health and Human Services, Public Health Service, Alcohol, Drug Abuse, and Mental Health Administration, National Institute on Drug Abuse, Washington, 1992.

Lichtblau, Eric. "Crime Down for 8th Year, FBI Reports." *The Los Angeles Times*. Vol. CXX. No. 318, 16 Oct. 2000. A10.

Light, Ken. *Texas Death Row*. Photographs by Ken Light, essay by Suzanne Donovan. Jackson, MS: University Press of Mississippi, 1997.

Lipsitz, George. *American Studies in a Moment of Danger*. Minneapolis and London: University of Minnesota Press, 2001.

———. *The Possessive Investment in Whiteness: How White People Profit from Identity Politics*. Philadelphia: Temple University Press, 1998.

Lyon, David. *The Electronic Eye: The Rise of Surveillance Society*. Minneapolis: University of Minnesota Press, 1994.

———. "An electronic panopticon? A sociological critique of surveillance theory." *The Sociological Review*. Vol. 41, No. 4. November 1993, 653–678.

———. *Surveillance Society: Monitoring everyday Life*. Issues in Society. Series editor Tim May. Buckingham and Philadelphia: Open University Press, 2001.

McCall, Nathan. *Makes Me Wanna Holler: A Young Black Man in America*. New York: Random House, 1994.

The Mack. Dir. Michael Campus. Cinema Releasing Corporation, 1973.

Maguire, Kathleen and Ann L. Pastore. *Sourcebook of Criminal Justice Statistics—1996*. Washington, D.C.: U.S. Government Printing Office, 1997.

Mahan, Sue. "Co-Corrections: Doing Time Together." *Corrections Today*. Aug. 1986, Vol. 48, No. 6, pp. 136, 138, 140, 164–165.

Malcolm X and Alex Haley. *The Autobiography of Malcolm X*. 1964. New York: Ballantine, 1992.

Martin, Dannie M. *In the Hat*. New York: Simon and Schuster, 1997.

Massey, James. *Doing Time in American Prisons: A Study of Modern Novels*. New York and Westport, CN: Greenwood Press, 1989.

Masters, Jarvis Jay. *Finding Freedom: Writings from Death Row.* Junction City, CA: Padma Publishing, 1997.

Mathiesen, Thomas. *Prison on Trial: A Critical Assessment.* London and Newbury Park, CA: SAGE Publications, 1990.

Mauer, Marc. "Blacks and the System." *The Angolite.* May/June 1999. Vol. 24, No. 3. 28–38.

———. *Race to Incarcerate.* The Sentencing Project. New York: New Press, 1999.

———. *Young Black Men and the Criminal Justice System: A Growing National Problem.* Washington, D.C.: The Sentencing Project, 1990.

Mercer, Kobena. *Welcome to the Jungle: New Positions in Black Cultural Studies.* New York and London: Routledge, 1994.

Metropolis. Dir. Fritz Lang. Paramount Pictures, 1926.

Miller, Stephen Paul. *The Seventies Now: Culture as Surveillance.* New Americanists. Series editor Donald E. Pease. Durham and London: Duke University Press, 1999.

Millgate, Michael. *American Social Fiction: James to Cozzens.* Edinburgh and London: Oliver and Boyd, 1964.

MIM (Maoist Internationalist Movement). "Not Down for the Lockdown: Fight against Super-jail for Kids Advances." *Newsletter.* Email. 10 Aug. 2001.

Mirandé, Alfredo. *Gringo Justice.* Notre Dame, IN: University of Notre Dame Press, 1987.

Muller, Judy. "Preventing Prison Rape." *ABC World News Tonight.* 18 April 2001. <http://more.abcnews.go.com/sections/wnt/worldnewstonight/wnt010418_prisonrape3_feature.html>.

Mulvey, Laura. *Visual and Other Pleasures.* Bloomington, IN: Indiana University Press, 1989.

No Escape. Dir. Martin Campbell. HBO Home Video, 1994.

O Brother, Where Art Thou? Dir. Joel Coen. Buena Vista Pictures, 2000.

Olney, James, ed. *Autobiography: Essays Theoretical and Critical.* Princeton, NJ: Princeton University Press, 1980.

Omi, Michael and Howard Winant. *Racial Formation in the United States: From the 1960s to the 1990s.* Second edition. New York and London: Routledge, 1994.

Oshinsky, David M. *"Worse Than Slavery": Parchman Farm and the Ordeal of Jim Crow Justice.* New York and London: Free Press, 1996.

Ostfeld, Adrian M. et al. *Stress, Crowding, and Blood Pressure in Prison.* Environment and Health Series. Hillsdale, NJ: L. Erlbaum Associates, 1987.

Oz. HBO. 2001.

Paasewe, Khandi, Rev. *New Afrikan Independence Movement.* 17 July 2001. <http://www.netset.com/~khandi/pgrna1.htm>.

Palmer, Gareth. "The New Spectacle of Crime." *Cybercrime: Law Enforcement, Security and Surveillance in the Information Age.* Eds. Douglas Thomas and Brian D. Loader. London and New York: Routledge, 2000. 85–102.

Parenti, Christian. *Lockdown America: Police and Prisons in the Age of Crisis.* London and New York: Verso, 1999.

Parish, James Robert. *Prison Pictures from Hollywood: Plots, Critiques, Casts and Credits for 293 Theatrical and Made-for-Television Releases.* Jefferson, NC and London: McFarland and Co., 1991.

Peltier, Leonard. *Prison Writings: My Life Is My Sun Dance*. Ed. Harvey Aden, introduction by Chief Arvol Looking Horse. New York: St. Martin's Press, 1999.

Penley, Constance. "Time Travel, Primal Scene, and the Critical Dystopia." *Close Encounters: Film, Feminism, and Science Fiction*. Eds. Constance Penley, Elisabeth Lyon, Lynn Spiegel, and Janet Bergstrom. Minneapolis, MN and Oxford: University of Minneapolis Press, 1991.

Perkins, Margo V. *Autobiography as Activism: Three Black Women of the Sixties*. Jackson, MS: University of Mississippi Press, 2000.

Petersen, Julie K. *Understanding Surveillance Technologies: Spy Devices, Their Origins and Applications*. Boca Raton, FL and London: CRC Press, 2001.

Piñero, Miguel. *Short Eyes*. New York: Hill and Wang, 1975.

"Prisons in the United States of America." *Human Rights Watch*. <http://www.hrw.org/advocacy/prisons/u-s.htm> 13 June 2002.

Public Enemy. "Black Steel and the Hour of Chaos." <http://www.leoslyrics.com/listlyrics>. 27 Oct. 2002.

Puig, Manuel. *Kiss of the Spider Woman*. 1976. Trans. Thomas Colchie. New York: Random House, 1980.

Reed, Ishmael. Preface to Eldridge Cleaver's *Soul on Ice*. 1968. New York: Bantam Doubleday Dell, 1992.

Reitz, Kevin R. "Sentencing." *The Handbook of Crime and Punishment*. Ed. Michael Tonry. New York and Oxford: Oxford University Press, 1998. 542–562.

Remple, Allison. Unpublished essay, 2002.

Rideau, Wilbert and Ron Wikberg, eds. *Life Sentences: Rage and Survival Behind Bars*. New York: Random House, 1992.

Rose, Tricia. *Black Noise: Rap Music and Black Culture in Contemporary America*. Hanover, NH and London: University Press of New England, 1994.

Rosenblatt, Roger. "Black Autobiography: Life as the Death Weapon." *Autobiography: Essays Theoretical and Critical*. Ed. James Olney. Princeton, NJ: Princeton University Press, 1980. 169–180.

Ross, Andrew. "Cowboys, Cadillacs and Cosmonauts: Families, Film Genre, and Technocultures." *Engendering Men*. Eds. Boone, Joseph A. and Michael Cadden. New York: Routledge, 1990.

Sabo, Don, Terry A. Kupers, and Willie London, eds. *Prison Masculinities*. Philadelphia: Temple University Press, 2001.

Salas, Floyd. *Tattoo the Wicked Cross*. 1967. Sagaponack, NY: Second Chance Press, 1981.

Sandoval, Chela. *Methodology of the Oppressed*. Minneapolis and London: University of Minnesota Press, 2000.

———. "New Sciences: Cyborg Feminism and the Methodology of the Oppressed." *Cybersexualities: A Reader on Feminist Theory, Cyborgs, and Cyberspace*. Ed. Jenny Wolmark. Edinburgh: Edinburgh University Press, 2000.

Santa Barbara County Sheriff. <http://www.sbsheriff.org>. 28 Sept. 2001.

"Sanyika Shakur." An interview with Sanyika Shakur by N. Kurshan. 6 May 1996. <http://www-unix.oit.umass.edu/~kastor/fallprogram/fall-shakur.html>. 17 July 2001.

Sartwell, Crispin. *Act Like You Know: African-American Autobiography and White Identity.* Chicago and London: University of Chicago Press, 1998.

Scientific American. "News Briefs: Death Defying." Feb. 2001. 16.

"Sears Pulls Benetton Contract After Taking Heat from Customers over Ads." *ABC-News.com.* <http://abcnews.go.com/wire/Business/ap20000217_380.html>. 17 Feb. 2000.

Segal, Lynne. *Slow Motion: Changing Masculinities, Changing Men.* London: Virago Press, 1990.

Shakur, Sanyika (a.k.a. Scott, Kody). *Monster: The Autobiography of an L.A. Gang Member.* New York: Atlantic Monthly Press, 1993.

The Shawshank Redemption. Dir. Frank Darabont. Columbia Pictures, 1994.

Silverman, Kaja. *Male Subjectivity at the Margins.* New York and London: Routledge, 1992.

Simon, Stephanie. "Benetton Sued Over Death Row Visits." *The Los Angeles Times.* 24 Feb. 2000. Vol. CXIX, No. 83. A5.

The Simpsons. Episode # 5F13. FOX. 22 March 1998.

Singer, Linda. *Erotic Welfare: Sexual Theory and Politics in the Age of Epidemic.* Ed. And introduced by Judith Butler and Maureen MacGrogan. New York and London: Routledge, 1993.

Smith, Sidonie. *Where I'm Bound: Patterns of Slavery and Freedom in Black American Autobiography.* Westport, CN and London: Greenwood Press, 1974.

Sourcebook of Criminal Justice Statistics 2000, page 488. Table 6.1 Adults on probation, in jail or prison, and on parole. United States, 1980–2000. 28 April 2002. <http://www.albany.edu/sourcebook/1995/pdf/t61.pdf>

Sourcebook of Criminal Justice Statistics 1999, page 484. Table 6.2 Estimated number of adults under correctional supervision. 28 June 2001. <http://www.albany.edu/sourcebook/1995/pdf/ t62.pdf>.

Stallybrass, Peter and Allon White. *The Politics and Poetics of Transgression.* London: Methuen, 1986.

Staples, William G. *The Culture of Surveillance: Discipline and Social Control in the United States.* Contemporary Social Issues. Series editor George Ritzer. New York: St. Martin's Press, 1997.

Star Trek VI: The Undiscovered Country. Dir. Nicholas Meyer. Paramount Home Video, 1991.

Stern, Vivien. *A Sin Against the Future: Imprisonment in the World.* Boston: Northeastern University Press, 1998.

Stir Crazy. Dir. Sidney Poitier. Columbia Pictures, 1980.

Stone, Albert E. *Autobiographical Occasions and Original Acts: Versions of American Identity from Henry Adams to Nate Shaw.* Philadelphia: University of Pennsylvania Press, 1982.

Stop Prisoner Rape. <http://www.spr.org/docs/whatis.html>. 25 May 2001.

"The Story of a Black Punk." Anonymous. *Stop Prisoner Rape.* <http://www.spr.org/docs/black.punk.html>. 25 May 2001.

Styron, William. "Introduction" to Edward Bunker's *Dog Eat Dog.* New York: St. Martin's Press, 1996.

———. "Introduction" to Edward Bunker's *Education of a Felon: A Memoir.* New York: St. Martin's Press, 2000.

Superfly. Dir. Gordon Parks, Jr. Warner Bros., 1972.

Terminal Island. Dir. Stephanie Rothman. Dimension, 1973.

"Thirteen inmates shot, one killed, by guards in prison riot." *ABCNews.com.* 24 Feb. 2001. <http://abcnews.go.com/wire/us/ap20000224_554.html>.

Thomas, Charles. "Prison is Funny." Unpublished essay, 2002.

Thomas, Kendall. "'Ain't Nothin' Like the Real Thing': Black Masculinity, Gay Sexuality, and the Jargon of Authenticity." *Representing Black Men.* Eds. Marcellus Blount and George P. Cunningham. New York and London: Routledge, 1996. 55–69.

Thomas, Piri. *Seven Long Times.* 1974. Houston, TX: Arte Público Press, 1994.

Tonry, Michael. "Crime and Punishment in America." *The Handbook of Crime and Punishment.* Ed. Michael Tonry. New York and Oxford: Oxford University Press, 1998. 3–30.

———., ed. *The Handbook of Crime and Punishment.* New York and Oxford: Oxford University Press, 1998.

———. "Harsh Times." *The Angolite.* January/February 2000. Vol. 25, No. 1. 26–33.

2Pac (Tupac Shakur). "16 on Death Row." Album, *R U Still Down (Remember Me).* <http://www.nycity.demon.co.uk/2pac/16ondeat.tx>. 11 Sept. 2001.

Twelve Monkeys. Dir. Terry Gilliam. Universal Pictures, 1995.

Useem, Bert and Peter Kimball, *States of Siege: U.S. Prison Riots, 1971–1986.* New York: Oxford University Press, 1989.

Valdez, Luis. *Zoot Suit and Other Plays.* Houston, Texas: Arte Público Press, 1992.

Von der Muhll, George. "The Political Element in Literature." *Reading Political Stories: Representations of Politics in Novels and Pictures.* Ed. Maureen Whitebrook. Lanham, MD: Rowman and Littlefield Publishers, 1992.

Washington, Jerome. *A Bright Spot on the Yard: Notes and Stories from a Prison Journal.* Trumansburg, NY: Crossing Press, 1981.

———. *Iron House: Stories from the Yard.* Fort Bragg, CA: QED Press, 1994.

"We, On Death Row." Oliviero Toscani, photographs. Ken Shulman, interviews. United Colors of Benetton. Supplement to *Talk* Magazine. Feb. 2000.

Weinstein, Corey and Eric Cummins. "The Crime of Punishment: Pelican Bay Maximum Security Prison." *Criminal Injustice: Confronting the Prison Crisis.* Ed. Elihu Rosenblatt. Boston: South End Press, 1996.

Werner, David R. *Joint Images: An Annotated Bibliography of Prison Fiction.* La Verne, CA: University of La Verne, 1990.

Whitaker, Reg. *The End of Privacy: How Total Surveillance Is Becoming a Reality.* New York: New Press, 1999.

Wideman, John Edgar. *Brothers and Keepers.* 1984. New York: Random House, Vintage, 1995.

———. "Introduction." Mumia Abu-Jamal's *Live from Death Row.* New York: Avon Books, 1996.

Wiegman, Robyn. *American Anatomies: Theorizing Race and Gender.* Durham and London: Duke University Press, 1995.

———. "Feminism, 'The Boyz,' and Other Matters Regarding the Male." *Screening the Male: Exploring Masculinities in Hollywood Cinema.* Eds. Steven

Cohan and Ina Rae Hark. London and New York: Routledge, 1993. 173–193.

Willocks, Tim. *Green River Rising*. London: Jonathan Cape, 1994.

Wilson, James Q. "Drugs and Crime." *Drugs and Crime*. Ed. Michael Tonry and James Q. Wilson. Chicago: University of Chicago Press, 1990.

Index